D0583887

Using Mixed Methods

SAGE has been part of the global academic community since 1965, supporting high quality research and learning that transforms society and our understanding of individuals, groups, and cultures. SAGE is the independent, innovative, natural home for authors, editors and societies who share our commitment and passion for the social sciences.

Find out more at: **www.sagepublications.com**

Using Mixed Methods:

Frameworks for an Integrated Methodology

David Plowright

Los Angeles | London | New Delhi
Singapore | Washington DC

© David Plowright 2011

First published 2011

Apart from any fair dealing for the purposes of
research or private study, or criticism or review, as
permitted under the Copyright, Designs and Patents Act
1988, this publication may be reproduced, stored or
transmitted in any form, or by any means, only with
the prior permission in writing of the publishers,
or in the case of reprographic reproduction, in accordance
with the terms of licences issued by the Copyright Licensing
Agency. Enquiries concerning reproduction outside those
terms should be sent to the publishers.

SAGE Publications Ltd
1 Oliver's Yard
55 City Road
London EC1Y 1SP

SAGE Publications Inc.
2455 Teller Road
Thousand Oaks, California 91320

SAGE Publications India Pvt Ltd
B 1/I 1 Mohan Cooperative Industrial Area
Mathura Road
New Delhi 110 044

SAGE Publications Asia-Pacific Pte Ltd
33 Pekin Street #02-01
Far East Square
Singapore 048763

Library of Congress Control Number 2010923182

British Library Cataloguing in Publication data

A catalogue record for this book is available from the British Library

ISBN 978-1-84860-107-9
ISBN 978-1-84860-108-6 (pbk)

Typeset by C&M Digitals (P) Ltd, Chennai, India
Printed in India at Replika Press Pvt Ltd
Printed on paper from sustainable resources

A massive thank you to Allison and Alexandra.
I couldn't have done it without you both.

Contents

Acknowledgements

The author and publisher would like to thank the following for granting permission to use copyright material:

Research Randomizer for Figure 4.1, screen shot of the Research Randomizer from the website www.randomizer.org

Surveymonkey for Figure 7.1, screen shot of an online questionnaire from the website www.surveymonkey.com

MozVolunteers for Figure 9.3, screenshot of the web page 'About us' from the website www.mozvolunteers.com

Cambridge University Press for Figure 11.1 from S. E. Toulmin (1958) *The Uses of Argument*. Cambridge: Cambridge University Press.

About the author

Dr. David Plowright, is an experienced lecturer, researcher, supervisor and examiner at masters and doctoral levels.

He is currently a lecturer in the Faculty of Educational Studies at the University of Hull. His research interests are focused on educational leadership and management, and he is currently undertaking research into school improvement in South Africa.

In addition to working in education, David managed his own research and communications consultancy for a number of years, working with a variety of private and public sector clients.

1

From mixed methods to an integrated methodology

> **This chapter will:**
>
> - provide an introduction to the Frameworks for an Integrated Methodology (FraIM)
> - explain how to carry out small-scale social and educational research using an integrated methodology
> - briefly describe the structure of the book.

Introduction

This book is about undertaking small-scale social and educational research. You will find it helpful if you are a post-graduate student or a third year undergraduate student who is required to carry out and report on a research project for your programme of study.

You will no doubt have read, or be currently reading, a number of other research methodology textbooks. You may be surprised at the confusing ideas you will have encountered in your reading. This is to be expected, since there is a lot of confusion associated with carrying out research! It wasn't always like this.

Many years ago (too many to remember exactly!) when I had just started a degree in psychology, I remember sitting in a formal lecture and being told by the tutor that 'as psychologists, we don't talk to the sociologists down the road'. We all laughed, although I'm not too sure that we fully understood the true import of the statement that we thought was meant as a joke. But we soon discovered that it *wasn't* a joke. The lecturer was deadly serious. Why? Because our BSc psychology course was located firmly in the science faculty and the BA sociology degree was in the arts faculty. Sociologists, we were told, were not scientists nor were their subject and methods of study based on a scientific paradigm that valued systematically manipulated, observable behaviour and careful, objective counting and measuring.

That early pronouncement has always stayed with me. It was my first experience of confronting what is still an ongoing debate in the social and behavioural sciences. It is the question of how we come to an understanding of the world in which we live and whether or not that understanding can be reliable and trustworthy.

For those fifty or so students (in those days undergraduate groups were not very large) sat on hard stone benches in that draughty lecture hall (and students were more tolerant of poor quality facilities) the arguments were simple. On the one hand was experimental or scientific behaviourism, while on the other was ... well, there was no other hand. Scientific method ruled, OK. Personal views and opinions counted for nothing, mainly because they *could not* be counted. As putative scientists, albeit behavioural scientists, we were expected to deal in facts. In the opening paragraph of Dickens's *Hard Times*, the character of Gradgrind firmly and unequivocally announces:

> Now what I want is Facts. Teach these boys and girls nothing but Facts. Facts alone are wanted in life. Plant nothing else and root out everything else. You can only form the minds of reasoning animals upon Facts; nothing else will be of any service to them. This is the principle on which I bring up my own children and this is the principle on which I bring up these children. Stick to Facts, sir! (Dickens, 2003: 74)

In this book, I have tried to steer a new course through the often treacherous waters that are home to many different facts but also many different ideas, views, perspectives, feelings and opinions.

Research methodology is not an easy subject to understand. Carrying out research is always fraught with difficulties. To help you, there are many different books from many different authors. They aim to explain the often complex issues associated with undertaking social and educational research. This present book adds to this list, but you may already be wondering whether or not we need another publication on research weighing down your bookshelf.

The answer is a firm 'yes', because this book takes a different approach, a different perspective to framing the research process and the underpinning principles that enable us to understand the decisions we make and the actions we take when carrying out research. This seems rather a bold claim. Perhaps you will eventually decide it *is* too bold a claim.

What you will find in this book is a synthesis of different ideas that you may well have come across already. There is nothing new in that, of course. What is new, however, is the way these different ideas are brought together under a new and innovative approach to conceptualising and thinking about research methodology. This new approach I have called the FraIM, which stands for: **Fra**meworks for an **I**ntegrated **M**ethodology.

Rejecting a traditional dichotomy

The FraIM rejects the traditional dichotomy between 'qualitative methods' and 'quantitative methods'. This, again in itself is not new. The practice of 'mixed methods' has been with us for some time now. In 2007 a new journal, the *Journal of Mixed Methods Research*, was launched. It challenged the still prevalent idea that different approaches to conceptualising and undertaking research cannot be used together. Various other publications, including for example, the *Handbook of Mixed Methods in Social and Behavioral Research* (Tashakkori and Teddlie, 2003) and Creswell and Plano Clark's (2007) *Designing and Conducting Mixed Methods Research*, have promoted the use of combining different approaches to undertaking research.

This book builds on those ideas and accepts, in principle, their appropriateness for carrying out the kind of research that the vast majority of students will be undertaking for their courses. More importantly, however, the ideas in this book go beyond a mainstream mixed methods approach to research. It does this by taking a fresh look at the way we think about social and educational research. It rejects completely and emphatically the use of the terms and distinction between 'qualitative methods' and 'quantitative methods'. It even eschews the terms 'qualitative' and 'quantitative' for more useful and appropriate descriptions of the research process. You'll find that these words – the Q words – are not used again in this book, unless they appear in titles of publications to which I refer.

However, it is not just the words that are of significance here. It is the underlying concepts and meanings, expressed through those words, that channel our thoughts, actions and understanding. These are what the book is about and indeed the overall purpose is to invite you to think afresh about research.

Of course, you may not like the ideas you read about. You may find them too different or they may not fit your thinking about how research should be conceptualised or explained. I can only say: don't be too hasty in rejecting an invitation to take a fresh approach to your research.

So, what is the book about and why is the approach it introduces so different?

Frameworks

This book argues that we can use a series of 'frameworks' to structure our thinking about research. A framework can best be described as a basic structure that underlies a system, concept or text (Soanes and Stevenson, 2005). In a framework, there is no 'content', only structure. This means that a framework represents processes and activities in an abstract and generalised way. It can be seen as a model that describes the process of designing, planning and carrying out research. You're the one who supplies the 'content'. This is the focus of your scholarly interests and the methodological decisions you make and specific actions you take in your research.

Above all, the frameworks are aimed at supporting the *integration* of different elements of the research process to ensure the effective and successful study of social and educational phenomena. Integration here means to combine and structure the different elements of the process into a unified, coherent whole. Perhaps most important of all, it gives equal consideration to each element without privileging one element over any other.

The way this works will be explained in the rest of the book. You'll find that not everything about research is included. There is not the space to do this. This means that there will be some issues that are not covered. Others may be touched on only briefly. Some might be looked at in a fair amount of detail. The important thing to remember is that this book is an introductory text to using the FraIM. It lays out the groundwork, offers ideas about what an integrated methodology is and it provides an opportunity to apply those ideas to your own research.

The structure of the book

Chapter 2 introduces the FraIM and explains how you can use it as the basis of your research. It provides a brief outline of both the basic FraIM and the main, extended FraIM. The latter is an expansion of the former and provides a more detailed and comprehensive structure within which to work

Chapters 3 and 4 are about case selection. You'll discover that there are two stages in choosing the cases, or sources of data, for your research. The first is referred to as data source management and the second as integrated sampling. You may find the approach to data source management a little different from what you are familiar with.

Chapter 5 provides an introduction to methods of data collection and is an overview of the characteristics of the three methods that are part of the main FraIM. This is followed by chapters on each of the different methods. Chapter 6 focuses on observation, Chapter 7 on asking questions, and Chapters 8 and 9 on artefact analysis. You'll find some new and interesting ideas in these chapters, especially those concerned with integrating the different methods.

Chapter 10 is about data integration and challenges the current view about types of data used in research and the idea of data reduction.

Chapter 11 argues that the most appropriate approach to conceptualising the validity of research is to think in terms of the warrantability of research. This is not a new idea but is one that tends not to be referred to in most introductory texts. It is seen, however, as being appropriate for use with the FraIM.

The next two chapters are about ethicality in research. Chapter 12 concentrates on issues about participant-centred research and Chapter 13 looks at wider concerns associated with carrying out research based on the FraIM.

Chapter 14 tackles, perhaps all too briefly, the philosophical perspective – holistic integrationism – to which the FraIM refers. It is worth pointing out, even at this early stage, that you will be encouraged to reject the view that philosophy determines the methodology used in research. As an alternative, you'll be asked to consider that it is actually the other way round: methodology determines the philosophy we employ to help us understand and conceptualise the research process.

At the end of each chapter you'll find a section entitled 'associated reading', where a number of publications will be listed. However, because the FraIM is such a new idea you'll find that the reading is not explicitly or directly linked with the approach that is taken in this book. Inevitably, the publications will still take a traditional view about research or be firmly located within mainstream mixed methods research. However, please bear in mind that whatever you read, whoever you talk to, *you* are the one who is carrying out the research. It is *your* research and no matter how much advice or guidance you receive, *you* are the one who will make the decisions about what to do and about what actions to take. Most important of all, you will need to explain and justify the decisions you make. The chapters in this book aim to enable you to successfully achieve this.

Finally, this book was written in order to make a contribution to an interesting and fascinating process that will lead you to a clearer understanding of the principles, processes and procedures involved in research based on an integrated methodology.

Associated reading

- Bergman, M.M. (ed.) (2008) *Advances in Mixed Methods Research*. London: SAGE.
- Creswell, J.W. and Plano Clark, V.L. (2007) *Designing and Conducting Mixed Methods Research*. London: SAGE.
- Gorard, S. and Taylor, C. (2004) *Combining Methods in Educational and Social Research*. Maidenhead: Open University Press.
- Plano Clark, V.L. and Creswell, J. (2008) *The Mixed Methods Reader*. London: SAGE.
- Tashakkori, A. and Teddlie, C. (eds) (2003) *Handbook of Mixed Methods in Social and Behavioral Research*. London: SAGE.
- Teddlie, C. and Tashakkori, A. (2009) *Foundations of Mixed Methods Research: Integrating Quantitative and Qualitative Approaches in the Social and Behavioral Sciences*. London: SAGE.

2

The FraIM: Frameworks for an Integrated Methodology

This chapter will:

- introduce a number of selected issues about designing and planning your research
- describe and discuss the main stages in the FraIM
- provide examples of how to integrate data source management, methods of data collection and types of data used in research
- enable you to apply the FraIM to your own intended research.

Introduction

This chapter explains how the FraIM will help you structure your thinking about research and consequently enable you to integrate different approaches to each stage of the process.

The *Oxford Dictionary of English* defines a framework as 'a basic structure that underlies a system, concept or text' (Soanes and Stevenson, 2005: 685). The word 'framework' is often used as a synonym for 'model'. The basic model or framework that is proposed in this book for carrying out research is presented in Figure 2.1.

Similar structures or models can be found in, for example, Hammersley who distinguishes the 'selection of cases from at least four other aspects of research design: problem formulation; data collection; data analysis; and reporting the findings' (1992: 184). Punch (2009) draws on a simplified model of research which consists of:

- the *pre-empirical stage:* research area; topic; questions
- the *empirical stage:* design; data collection; data analysis; answer questions.

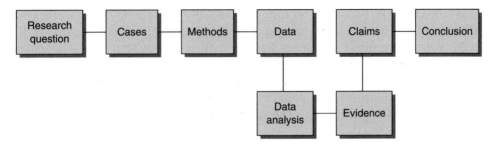

Figure 2.1   The basic structure of the FraIM

Punch explains that 'This view of research ... stresses the central role of research questions, and of systematically using empirical data to answer those questions' (2009: 10). The basic structure of the FraIM is also relatively straightforward, as with the above examples. It will help you carry out small-scale empirical investigations of educational and social issues. It is referred to as a framework because there is no 'content', only structure. This means that, like any model, it represents processes and activities in an abstract and gener-alised way. An advantage of using this approach is that the framework can be applied to any research project that you might want to undertake. It identifies the salient elements of the process and shows the links between each of the different elements.

The structure presented in Figure 2.1, however, is only the basic structure of the FraIM. As you read through this chapter and the rest of the book, you'll discover that there are frameworks within frameworks. They are, perhaps, a little like the Russian dolls you may be familiar with. A small doll is nested within a slightly larger doll and both are nested within the next larger sized doll and so on. All you see is the final, large doll. As you'll discover, that's what the FraIM is like. Figure 2.1 shows that there are a number of compo-nents or stages in the FraIM. The starting point, however, is the main research question and the process progresses through to the final conclusion.

Once you have decided what your question is, you will be in a position to make decisions about the choice of cases or participants, the methods of data collection to be used, the type of data to be collected and how the data will be analysed. Once the research is underway, the data will provide evidence for the claims you will make about the participants. In turn, this will enable you to reach conclusions about your research question.

Unlike most approaches to research, the FraIM does not dictate that you hold a particular philosophical position prior to beginning the research. It encourages a more responsive, flexible and open-minded attitude based on answering one or more research questions, finding a solution to a problem or addressing an important issue.

The integrated methodology framework, or FraIM, used here gives the impression that it is a linear process, with one stage following the next. At times, this will be true. At other times, there will be a process of iteration: you will move from one stage to the next and then back again. Sometimes you will make a decision about an earlier stage and then return to it as the research progresses and you amend your plans.

The important factor about the framework is that it functions to help your thinking, your planning and your activities. Most important of all, it acts as a template to guide you through the research process.

Explaining the FraIM

The following sections provide an outline explanation of each item of the FraIM. In places you may find that the explanation is fairly brief. However, please bear in mind that the purpose of the outline is to provide an overview, or sketch, of the FraIM and its constituent components. The detail comes in later chapters.

Figure 2.2 shows the addition of the different elements that make up each component of the basic FraIM. You'll find that further chapters refer regularly to this extended FraIM.

The research question

Each of the main items of the FraIM is an important element in the research process. In an integrated methodologies approach, the start of the process, however, is the main research question. The question is formulated within a number of different contexts. There are five contexts contingent to carrying out any research, although some will have more importance than others. These contexts are:

- professional
- organisational
- policy
- national
- theoretical.

Professional context

The professional context provides background information about you, the researcher. This includes what your job or professional role is. For example, if you are a full-time student or a head teacher then this will be part of the professional context of your research. This is information that, eventually, your readers are going to find helpful. For example, how long you have been in your present role? If you work in the health and social care sector, perhaps this is only your second or third year in the profession? This is the kind of information your readers will need to know. It will enable them to place your

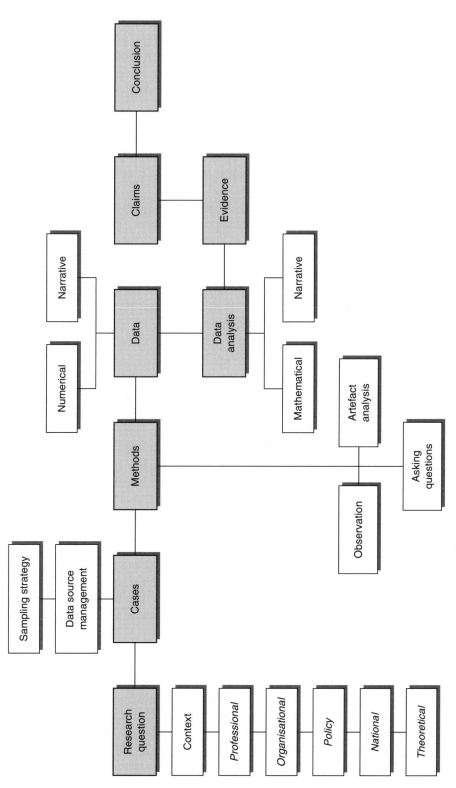

Figure 2.2 The main, extended FraIM

research in a personal and professional context, and help them to understand the potential professional perspective that you might have employed in your research. If say, you are researching students' use of the private study rooms in a university library, then your interest and perspective may be influenced by whether you are a student, a librarian or a member of the university's facilities/buildings department.

It will also be helpful to know why you have chosen a particular topic or subject as the focus of your research. Your previous experiences may have led you directly to your choice. Aspects of your current role may have informed your decision or it may be that a specific event has fired your enthusiasm about your research.

Whatever the source of your interest, being aware of the professional and personal context of your research enables you to answer the following question: out of all the possible topics you might have chosen, why did you choose this particular one? More importantly perhaps, it enables you to be aware of any potential biases you may have about your topic as a result of your previous experiences and perhaps long-held attitudes to the subject. These, in turn, may impact on the kind of questions that you ask in your research and how you interpret the findings.

Organisational context

Your research may take place in a particular organisational context. For example, it could be a small primary school in England. On this occasion, the number of pupils and teachers may have an impact on how you conduct your research and indeed what is possible, due to the size of the school. The organisational context, in this instance, may limit and restrict how you go about investigating your research question. On the other hand, it may provide opportunities that you wouldn't necessarily have if the school were a large secondary school. In a small school you might be able to carry out research into whole-school polices easier since staff may be more accessible, due to the smaller number in the school.

Different organisations have different cultures and it may be important for you to be aware of the nature of the culture in which your research will be undertaken. Knowing 'how we do things around here' enables any researcher to be more sensitive to what is acceptable or unacceptable when carrying out investigations in a particular organisational context. Of course, if you are already a member of the organisation, if you are a teacher in the school or say, a senior manager in a hospital where your research will take place, then you will already have some idea of the cultural nuances that exist there.

In addition, the organisational context may have an impact on the types of questions that you are able to ask in your research. The context may indeed even determine your research questions, even though you are *not* investigating the organisation as an organisation. Of course, if your research is not located in an organisation, then you will not need to take this element into consideration. For example, your research may require you to stop people in the street and ask them questions as part of a survey. It will be difficult to imagine what the organisational context would be in a case such as this!

Policy context

If your research draws directly on government policy, for example, the impact of Ofsted (the Office for Standards in Education) inspections on teacher morale in England, you will need to provide information about current, and probably past, policies relating to the Ofsted inspection process.

However, not all social and educational research is informed *directly* by policy and therefore it may not be necessary, nor helpful, to place your research in a policy context. For example, you may be interested in investigating the links between emotional intelligence and confidence in young adults. Here, the focus of the research would not necessarily benefit from an examination of, for example, the UK's *Every Child Matters* (DfES, 2003) agenda that gives pupils more say in evaluating their experiences of school.

Taking the policy context into consideration will inform your understanding of the issues you are investigating by giving you a wider and better informed perspective. It should also help you formulate more appropriate research questions since being familiar with the relevant policy publications will enable you to identify what issues are associated with those particular policies. Even if your research does not appear to be embedded in an explicit policy context, then you may want to consider Clough and Nutbrown's argument that 'all social research takes place in policy contexts of one form or another' (2002: 12).

National context

It may seem strange to include a recommendation that you take into account the national context of your research. Again, this may not apply to all research that you might carry out. However, your readers may not be from the same country as you, therefore it's unlikely that they will understand the national context within which your research will be conducted. For example, if the location of your research is in a university, say, in China, then it's doubtful if your readers will have much, if any, knowledge of the university system in that country. You will need to provide some background information about how higher education in China is structured and organised.

Not all research needs to *explicitly* take into account the national context. However, we are living through a massive expansion of globalised communication where, increasingly, we are expected at all levels and in all subjects to bear in mind that what happens in one part of the world can impact on other parts. In addition, research reports in journals or books frequently have an international audience. That audience will need some information about the national characteristics of the location in which the research was conducted. This might include the structures, the culture and the history of the particular aspect that you are researching. It will provide the national context for your investigation and this is something that you will intuitively be aware of if you are researching in your own country and culture. Others won't have that same awareness!

As with the policy context to your research, the national context may partly determine the research questions you ask, even if those questions are derived from a theoretical perspective. For example, your research may be looking at the theoretical issue of identity and be located in a poor, rural area of South Africa (Plowright and Plowright, 2008). It would be important to provide the national context to research of this nature since it is directly linked to the focus of the research. Furthermore, being aware of the national context may encourage you to consider how your research issues are investigated and reported on in other countries and other cultures.

Theoretical context

This is conventionally referred to as the *conceptual framework*. It is based on a search and review of relevant and appropriate literature that is focused on the substantive topic of your research. It starts with a literature search that involves collecting and reading a range of publications on your chosen topic or subject. It shows you what other authors, academics and researchers have written about the area and, as Trafford and Leshem point out, 'Their ideas will have given you theoretical perspectives that can guide your thinking about exactly what it is that you will investigate' (2008: 44).

As a result of carrying out a literature review, you will be well placed to develop and construct a conceptual framework that will be used to organise the underpinning ideas and theories in your research. Generally speaking, students find this one of the most challenging tasks in research. Burgess, Sieminski and Arthur explain that 'One of the difficulties you, as a researcher face, is to disentangle the numerous theoretical points of view you come across and make sense of these for your own research' (2006: 41). It is essential, therefore, that you start undertaking a literature search and review as soon as possible!

It's likely, of course, that you will start your research with a fair amount of reading already completed. This will probably come from the other parts of your study programme or even earlier if you have recently completed a previous degree. The advice usually given at the beginning of a dissertation or thesis is that you should choose a topic and a research question that:

1 is in an area that you have already spent some time studying or thinking about
2 but one that takes you out of your comfort zone.

If you have already spent time studying your topic, then you will have completed some reading and will have started to develop an understanding of what some of the important issues are. But there is no point in carrying out research that does not challenge you and stretch your abilities: as they say – no pain, no gain!

Balance

The balance, emphasis and relevance of each of the different contexts will change as a result of the overall situation in which research is conducted.

At times, the professional/personal context may be important since your research might be based on your own past or current experience. At other times, the organisational context will be a priority, especially if your research is about the finances of the organisation. The national context may play only a small role in your thinking as you formulate your research question and carry out the subsequent research. At other times, it may be very important to take the national context into account, especially if you are undertaking a comparative study of, say, management issues in two hospitals.

Whatever the focus of your interests, there will always be contextual factors that come into play and these need to be considered as you start on your research.

Justification for your research question

There is another important factor that you need to be aware of when you start to plan your research. The different contexts will provide you with a justification for your research question. For example, as a result of your *professional* experience of, say, working in a further education college, you may have identified a specific problem with the college's quality assurance procedures related to collecting feedback from students about their learning experiences.

Imagine that, as part of your middle management responsibilities in cross-college quality committee meetings you have continually asked: 'Why are there problems with collecting and collating formative evaluation feedback from students throughout the college, in order to ensure that continuous improvement is ongoing?' No one seems to have an answer to your question! It is something that needs addressing urgently, since it is likely that the college will be inspected very soon. However, up to now, you have not had the opportunity to investigate what can be done to improve such procedures in your organisation. Consequently, you have now decided that you will focus on this issue for your research.

You are already aware of the pressures that management of the college are under in terms of the *policy* requirements from the funding bodies and inspection services. You have lived with these for some time. You know, therefore, where to access information about what is needed to meet the government's accountability agenda through the college's quality enhancement regime. These also include the legal requirements at *national* level to which all further education colleges in England (UK) are subject.

After having undertaken some reading as part of your literature search, you begin to develop an understanding of the *theoretical* issues associated with, say, change management. These will help you to conceptualise the changes that might be needed to improve the quality assurance systems in the college. So, as you think through your intended research, you begin to realise that your research question is firmly placed in a number of contexts.

☐ Summary 2.1

- Your research will start with a clearly expressed research question.
- It will be formulated in relation to:

  - the professional context within which your research will be carried out
  - your own personal interests and professional role
  - the organisational context which may limit the kind of research you will carry out
  - a policy context which may have a direct or indirect impact on your research
  - a national context
  - a theoretical context that provides the conceptual framework of your research.

The cases

Once you have formulated your research question, it will be clear that your research will involve one or more sources of information. These sources will provide you with the data for your research. Hammersley (1992) argues for the use of the term 'cases' to describe the sources of data and these can range from individuals to organisations or international social systems. In some analytical software, including the commonly used SPSS (Statistical Package for the Social Sciences) the term 'case' is also used to refer to the data sources. More conventionally, when sources of data are individuals, they are usually referred to as participants, respondents or informants.

The term 'cases', however, seems to capture the wide range and variety of data sources that are used in research. These can vary from, say, pupils being aggressive in the playground to organisations with different cultural identities. In the former, the cases are the pupils and in the latter, the organisations. On the other hand, cases might refer to inanimate objects. For example, in a study of graffiti in bus shelters, you might be interested in the messages that are scratched and written on the walls of the shelters. The cases, in this instance, would be either the shelters or the walls.

Selection of cases takes place at two levels: the first level can be referred to as data source management and the second as sampling decisions. The first level involves deciding on which approaches are to be used for managing the sources of data. The choice is:

- case study
- experiment
- survey
  (Hammersley, 1992: 184).

Chapter 3 will explain and discuss, in some detail, the criteria on which data source management is based. It will do this by discussing the similarities and differences between case studies, experiments and surveys. This approach may appear somewhat unusual, especially if you are already familiar with using terms such as 'participants' or 'respondents'. Well, this is a different approach to thinking about how to approach your research!

Although the next chapter provides detailed information about data source management, it will be helpful to mention here that there are three criteria to consider in the decision-making process about how to organise your cases. These are:

- the number of cases in your research
- the degree of control you, as the researcher, have over which cases are allocated to which groups
- the degree of naturalness, that is, the ecological validity, of the groupings.

In keeping with the focus of this book – that of integrating different approaches at all stages in the research process – it will explain, with examples, how you can use a combination of different data source management procedures in your research.

Sampling decisions

Once you have decided which approach to data source management is appropriate for your research, you will need to make a decision about sampling. Sampling decisions determine which cases to include in your research. The cases will be allocated to the groups resulting from your data source management decision.

The same process of making sampling decisions can be used for case studies, experiments and surveys, and Chapter 4 will explain this process more fully.

Methods of data collection

By now, you will have formulated your research question, taking into account the contexts within which your research will be planned and undertaken. You will also have made a decision about how you will approach the task of data source management and how you will select your cases through one or more sampling decisions. It is now time to consider how you will collect the data from your cases.

Research based on the FraIM argues that there are three types of methods of data generation and collection:

- observation
- asking questions
- artefact analysis.

It may appear unusual that all data collection can be subsumed under these three headings. However, there is a logic and persuasiveness about such an approach. An explanation of the underlying rationale for this will be provided in some depth in Chapter 5. For the moment, since you are still in the preliminary stages of thinking through your research, it will be sufficient to briefly describe the main characteristics of the choices open to you.

Observation can include covert or overt observing of behaviour. This can include audio-recording of discussion and verbal interchanges. It could be, for example, the observation of non-verbal behaviour or hand-raising by pupils when answering questions in a school classroom.

Asking questions can involve carrying out interviews with your respondents. These might be highly structured using an interview schedule or they may be semi-structured interviews, based on an interview guide that lists only areas for discussion. However, it may be more appropriate to use a far less structured approach in order to explore interviewees' feelings about, say, the level of stress they experience in the workplace. Asking questions can also involve using a written, self-completion questionnaire containing open-ended and/or closed questions. More detail is provided in Chapter 7 including the increasing use of communications technology to ask questions.

Artefact analysis refers to objects or events that are produced by people. These might be radio and TV programmes or advertisements; they could be publicity brochures produced by a university or a school or a business organisation. They may be diaries produced by schoolchildren about their experiences of holiday adventures. They also include theatre, dance, food and drink. The type of artefacts that are data sources for research is based partly on the senses but also includes examples of text-based artefacts and what can be referred to as a kinaesthetic/spatial dimension. These are discussed later in some detail in Chapters 8 and 9.

Choice of methods

Your choice of method will be characterised by the following:

- the degree of structure
- the level of mediation, that is, the proximal/distal location of the researcher in relation to the issues under study.

The *degree of structure* of data collection methods will determine the level of pre-structuring of the data collected. This has implications, therefore, for the way that data are generated, collected and analysed. This will be explained fully and in detail in Chapter 5 which will also explain the criteria on which degree of structure is based.

The *level of mediation* is no less important than the idea of structure in deciding on how appropriate a method of data collection might be. For example, when comparing asking questions and observations, the former tend to be at a relatively high level of mediation. On the other hand, observations tend to be at a relatively low level of mediation. The researcher is usually physically and temporally closer to the phenomena being studied.

Different levels of mediation and degree of structure in research methods raise different issues when carrying out research informed by the integrated methodology of the FraIM. For example, they create different potential sources of error and bias for the research. These will be explained and discussed in some detail in the following chapters. For the moment, as you plan and design your research, you will be considering which methods of data collection you will use. You will need to take into account the aims of your research; the purpose of the research, who or what the cases are and, of course, the research question.

Summary 2.2

- The term 'cases' refers to the sources of data for your research.
- Selection of cases takes place at two levels: data source management and sampling decisions.
- Strategies for managing the sources of data include case study, experiment and survey.
- Criteria for choice of data source management are:

    – the number of cases in the research
    – the degree of control the researcher has over which cases are allocated to which groups
    – the degree of naturalness, that is, the ecological validity, of the groupings.

- Sampling decisions determine which cases to include in your research.
- There are three types of methods of data generation and collection: observation, asking questions and artefact analysis.
- Choice of method will be partly characterised by two criteria: degree of structure and level of mediation.

Data

The next stage in the FraIM concerns the data you will collect in your research. There are two categories of data: numerical and narrative. When you collect numerical data, you will be interested in counting and measuring. You will be dealing with numerical information about the issues you are studying. The data are often seen as unambiguous, fixed and drawing on the use of the logical code of mathematics.

Narrative data deal with words and media texts, that is, still and moving imagery, rather than numbers. The data are very often experienced as ambiguous. They have meanings that are fluid and often contentious, with more opportunities for different interpretations, depending on a range of factors, including the context and the people involved. Narrative data draw on conventional codes of meaning that are based on the use of language or visual or auditory imagery, with all their complexities and ambiguities.

Each type of data has further characteristics that will be explained in more detail later. You'll find that each has advantages and disadvantages and different functions and purposes. As you plan your research, at this stage you will need to consider what type of data you will collect.

Data analysis

The next stage in the planning process is to determine how you will analyse your data. If you took a relatively traditional approach to research, you would probably be looking forward to using mathematical and statistical analyses for numerical data and, say, theme analysis for narrative data. However, you may not want to restrict yourself to such approaches. You may want to turn your narrative data into numerical information and describe your numerical data with the use of narrative.

A synthesis

You are now in a position to start the process of integrating the different components of the FraIM. This initial integration will focus primarily on the cases, methods of data collection and types of data leading to the three dimensional model shown in Figure 2.3.

The first, rather obvious, point to note is that there are eighteen cells in the model. Each cell represents a combination of each of the three elements from the FraIM. Any or all of the cells are a permissible combination when undertaking research, although to cover all cells would be a mammoth undertaking!

Tables 2.1 and 2.2 provide examples that draw on the use of, respectively, numerical and narrative data. The tables outline a number of imagined research projects where the main research question might be: 'What are the salient factors associated with girls' aggressive behaviour in a rural primary school?' In addition, there will also be a number of sub-questions that the research will focus on. Table 2.1 consists of cells 1 to 9 from the model, which cover the collection of numerical data aimed at contributing to answering the main research question.

Table 2.2, consists of cells 10 to 18, which cover the collection of narrative data. First, the examples in both tables are a very brief demonstration that case selection, methods of data collection and types of data can be effectively combined. Second, they show that both numerical and narrative data can be collected using the same methods, that is, asking questions, observing and analysing artefacts. Further, they also show that, contrary to what some researchers argue, numerical data can be employed, for example, when a case study is used and narrative data can be collected using an experimental approach.

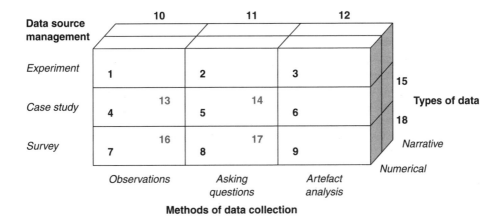

Figure 2.3   Simple three-dimensional model of an integrated approach to designing research

Table 2.1   Research using numerical data

	Methods of data collection		
	Observations	**Asking questions**	**Artefact analysis**
Experiment	**Cell 1** Numerical data are collected as a result of observing aggressive behaviour in a school playground under different conditions. There are two conditions: (1) boys and girls segregated (2) boys and girls not segregated.	**Cell 2** An interview schedule, based on a Likert scale, is used to collect numerical data about how often a number of selected boys and girls witness aggressive behaviour during segregated and nonsegregated playground time.	**Cell 3** Numerical data are collected as a result of analysing pupils' diaries about aggressive behaviour in a school playground under different conditions of gendered segregation and non-segregation.
Case study	**Cell 4** Numerical data are collected using a checklist of the occurrence of aggressive behaviours in the playground from one group of girls at one case study primary school.	**Cell 5** An interview schedule, based on a Likert scale, is used to collect numerical data when interviewing a small group of particularly aggressive girls in a primary school.	**Cell 6** Numerical data are collected as a result of analysing the written stories and diaries of a small case study group of particularly aggressive girls about behaviour in a primary school playground.
Survey	**Cell 7** Numerical data, using a rating scale, are collected using observations of a sample of lessons to determine the level of aggressive behaviour of pupils.	**Cell 8** Using an interview schedule, based on a Likert scale, a sample of parents are interviewed about known incidences of aggressive behaviour in a primary school.	**Cell 9** Using a structured coding schedule, a sample of letters from parents is analysed for the number of complaints that are made about aggressive behaviour in a primary school.

Table 2.2   Research using narrative data

	Methods of data collection		
	Observations	**Asking questions**	**Artefact analysis**
Experiment	**Cell 10** Narrative data are collected as a result of observing behaviour in a school playground under different conditions. There are two conditions: (1) boys and girls segregated (2) boys and girls not segregated.	**Cell 11** Interviews are carried out, using open-ended questions, about how boys and girls feel about segregated and non-segregated playground time.	**Cell 12** Pupils' visual artwork, about the topic of aggressive behaviour in a school playground, is analysed and related to different conditions of gender segregation.
Case study	**Cell 13** Narrative data are collected using a less structured approach to observing the occurrence of aggressive behaviours in the playground at one case study primary school.	**Cell 14** Interviews are carried out with a small group of particularly aggressive girls in a primary school aimed at trying to understand their perceptions of aggression on friendship issues.	**Cell 15** The recorded and transcribed informal classroom conversations of a small group of girls in a primary school are analysed using discourse analysis.
Survey	**Cell 16** Narrative data are collected, using a less structured approach to observing a sample of lessons to determine the level of pupils' aggressive behaviour.	**Cell 17** A sample of parents is interviewed using open-ended questions, about their views of the level of aggressive behaviour in a primary school.	**Cell 18** A survey is undertaken of material placed on notice boards and display boards throughout a primary school to determine if they present aggressive attitudes and behaviour.

Summary 2.3

- There are two types of data: numerical and narrative.
- Numerical data are generated as a result of counting and measuring.
- Narrative data deal with words and media texts, that is, still and moving imagery.
- There is no necessity to restrict data processing to mathematically analysing numerical data and using narrative analysis for narrative data.
- Narrative data can be transformed into numerical information and numerical data can be described using narrative.
- Eighteen different research strategies can be generated by integrating case selection strategy, methods of data collection and types of data.
- Both numerical and narrative data can be collected using the same methods of data collection.

Conclusion

This chapter has outlined a number of basic issues that you need to consider when starting to design and plan your research based on the FraIM. It has provided an overall, general introduction to the framework by outlining the main elements of the FraIM. These are the research question and the context within which the research will be undertaken; the data source management and the sampling decisions underlying the case selection strategy; the methods of data collection you intend to use; the types of data you will collect and the analyses of those data. In addition, there has been an opportunity to see how the FraIM can be applied to your own proposed research.

This chapter has argued that it is possible to use and integrate different combinations of data sources, methods and types of data as part of a research project. The chapter has introduced a different way of thinking about categorising the sources of data for research and describing the types of data that can be collected. Further, the chapter also explained that there is a choice in the way you analyse your data.

The next chapter starts the process of looking in some detail at the elements within the FraIM, beginning with data source management.

 Reflections

1 To what extent is the FraIM different to the approaches to research you have previously encountered?
2 Draw out the main, extended FraIM and fit your own research into each of the components.
3 How useful do you find the FraIM in helping you think through your research?
4 Is there anything missing from the FraIM that you think should be included?

Associated reading

- Bergman, M.M. (ed.) (2008) *Advances in Mixed Methods Research*. London: SAGE. See Chapter 1, 'The straw men of the qualitative–quantitative divide and their influence on mixed methods research'.
- Blaikie, N. (2000) *Designing Social Research*. Cambridge: Polity. See Chapter 3, 'Research questions and objectives'.
- Blaxter, L., Hughes, C. and Tight, M. (2006) *How to Research* (3rd edn). Maidenhead: Open University Press. See Chapter 2, 'Getting started'.
- Bourner, T. (1996) 'The research process: four steps to success', Chapter 2 in T. Greenfield (ed.), *Research Methods: Guidance for Postgraduates*. London: Arnold.

- Creswell, J. (2003) *Research Design: Qualitative, Quantitative and Mixed Methods Approaches* (2nd edn). London: SAGE. See Chapter 6, 'Research questions and hypotheses'.
- Punch, K.F. (2009) *Introduction to Research Methods in Education.* London: SAGE. See Chapter 4, 'Research questions'.
- Knight, P. (2002) *Small-Scale Research.* London: SAGE. See Chapter 1, 'Starting with writing'.
- Teddlie, C. and Tashakkori, A. (2009) *Foundations of Mixed Methods Research: Integrating Quantitative and Qualitative Approaches in the Social and Behavioral Sciences.* London: SAGE. See Chapter 6, 'Generating questions in mixed methods research'.

3

Case selection: data source management

This chapter will:

- **clarify the criteria on which data source management is based**
- **illustrate the similarities and differences between case study, experiment and survey as the basis of data source management**
- **explain when to use case study, experiment and survey in research**
- **enable you to apply the principles of integrated data source management to your own intended research.**

Introduction

This chapter looks in more detail at the process of data source management which is the first stage of the case selection procedure in the FraIM. The second stage requires you to make sampling decisions and this is covered in the next chapter.

You may want to refresh your memory about where data source management appears in the FraIM by referring to Figure 2.2 in Chapter 2.

It was pointed out in the previous chapter that Hammersley (1992) argues for the use of the term 'cases' to describe the sources of data. Remember, too, that cases need not necessarily be individuals or organisations. They can be objects such as desks in a school, bus shelters or notice boards in a building. Using desks as cases might be part of a research study that is investigating the incidences of graffiti in a school. As was mentioned in the previous chapter, this might also apply, for example, to a study of bus shelters. Another example might be a study of notice boards in an organisation, as part of a research investigation into the style of the information pinned to notice boards.

Data sources

When you start to plan and carry out research, your research question will help to determine what your sources of data will be. You'll remember from the previous chapter that these can be organised into the following categories:

- case study
- experiment
- survey.

There are a number of characteristics that identify each category. Three stand out above the others. These are:

- the number of cases in your research
- the degree of control you, as the researcher, have over which cases are allocated to which groups
- the degree of naturalness, that is, ecological validity, of the groupings.

These characteristics, however, should be seen as *dimensions* or *continua* on which case study, experiment and survey will lie.

It is important not to lose sight of the fact that you can, of course, use a combination of different types of data source management strategies in your research.

Number of cases in your research

This may seem a rather trivial factor to take into account in your research, but imagine planning to carry out a thousand in-depth interviews, lasting up to two hours each, from different regions of the country! Without considerable financial and human resources, this would be an impossible task, so number of cases really is very important!

A case study is a study of a single case and is associated with one or very few participants (Bryman, 2008). At the other end of the dimension, a survey can involve a relatively large number of cases and is 'efficient in terms of being able to gather large amounts of data at reasonably low cost and effort' (Muijs, 2004: 44). Generally speaking, an experiment will consist of a few to many cases although experiments can be carried out with single participants, for example on patients who suffer from rare brain damage (Coolican, 2004: 70).

You will already no doubt be thinking about the terms 'few', 'many' and 'considerable'. It is easy to determine what the extremes are: that is, one or a thousand. But the difficulties arise when we look at the border between, say, 'few' and 'many'. The use of these words also suggests that the categories over-lap. In fact, there is a continuum, from a single case study to large survey, with experiment lying between the two. At some point, a case study can be treated as an experiment, as long as the other technical conditions of experimentation are met. Likewise, an experiment can be seen as a survey, in terms of numbers, given that the case selection meets the other conditions of degree of control and ecological validity.

Please bear in mind that exact and precise counting is not being used here. You will draw on the number of cases as a guide, in order to make appropriate decisions about your research. You are not dealing with precision. That means you are left to make a judgement, a professional judgement as a researcher, about issues such as this one.

Furthermore, an answer about whether or not you should use case study, experiment or survey will become clearer when you have considered the other criteria associated with data source management. For the moment, the important point to be made here is that when planning and designing your research – and even more importantly, when carrying out research – you will need to take into account the number of cases that are your data sources. This is because there are important issues associated with the numbers of cases in research. These are, on the one hand, methodological and on the other, logistical.

Methodological issues

Methodological issues include the amount of in-depth detail that can be collected from the cases and the degree of generalisability that can be made about the inferences from the data collection. These are briefly outlined in Table 3.1.

With limited resources, including the amount of time you have, it follows that the amount of detail that can be collected will be limited by the number of cases on which your research is based. The more cases you draw on for your data, the more limited you will be in the amount of in-depth information you will be able to collect. In a case study, for example, there 'is a concentration of the specific rather than the general – a choice of depth over breadth' (Burton, Brundrett and Jones, 2008: 66–7).

Table 3.1 Methodological issues associated with numbers of cases employed in research

	One to a few cases	Few to many cases	Many to a considerably large number of cases
Amount of detail	Large amount of in-depth detail can be collected about the case(s).	Less in-depth detail can be collected about the cases.	Limited amount of detail can be collected about the cases. Information tends to be relatively superficial.
Degree of generalisability	Generalisability is limited and restricted.	Generalisability is more achievable if there are many cases.	Generalisability is possible if there are a large number of cases.

Generalisability is perhaps not quite so straightforward. It involves arriving at justified, or warrantable, claims about the participants in your study and then applying those claims to a wider group that the participants represent or were drawn from. However, the fewer the cases, the more restricted is your opportunity to generalise or relate the findings to a wider population. It is important to recognise, however, that not only does generalisability depend on the number of cases in your research but it also relies partly on the technicalities of different types of sampling. This will be covered in more detail in the next chapter.

Logistical issues

Logistical issues associated with the number of cases in your research are associated mainly with the location of your participants. The fewer the cases and the fewer the geographical locations, the easier it will be to contact the participants and undertake the data collection. If you have a potentially large number of participants, then depending on your methods of data collection, it may be difficult and expensive to collect the data. This is especially the case if you intend to collect narrative data face to face with your informants.

If you intend to collect numerical data, then a survey using a printed questionnaire or a set of questions distributed via email would make the research more manageable. It would certainly be more cost-effective. However, even these approaches have their practical difficulties, since you will be sending a high volume of information out and (hopefully) receiving a large amount of information in return. You'll need to think these issues through as you plan your research.

Degree of control

Degree of control relates to how much control you have over which cases are allocated to which group or groups in your research. Table 3.2 summarises the differences between case study, survey and experiment.

Case study

In a case study strategy, the researcher has limited, if any, control over case allocation. The researcher's choice is determined and limited by the potential case or cases that make up the group that will be studied.

A case study usually consists of one or a few participants. For example, as shown in Table 3.2, the case study may be the three deputy headteachers in a large secondary school. The only choice to consider here is which school is chosen and, of course, why. Whatever the reasons for the choice, there will only be the three deputy head teachers to select for the case study. Therefore, in this example, the researcher has no control over who is the target of study during the research, once the school has been selected.

Table 3.2 Degree of control

	Case study	Survey	Experiment
	Limited control in allocation of cases to case study	**Some control over allocation of cases to survey groups**	**High level of control when allocating cases to experimental and comparison or control groups**
	← ↓	↓	↓ →
Degree of control	The researcher's choice is determined and limited by the potential case or cases that make up the group or individual that will be studied.	Groups that already exist are chosen but the researcher has some control over which cases are selected from within those groups.	The cases are created partly by the researcher who has a high level of control over the criteria for creating the cases and which cases are allocated to which group.
Example	A case study of three deputy head teachers in a secondary school.	Questionnaire survey of a sample of teachers in a local authority area: total number of teachers = 600 and a 25% sample of 150 is taken.	A field experiment: a comparison of pupil views and standard of work during the introduction of project work in Years 7 and 8. Half the cohort undertake the new project work, half do not, in its first year of implementation.

Survey

Using a survey approach, groups that already exist are chosen for the research. The researcher may have *some* control, however, over which cases are selected to take part in the survey. He or she will also have a choice of which cases are selected from *within* those groups. In the example in Table 3.2, the schools in the local authority already exist, of course, but the researcher will decide which schools are chosen and which teachers within those schools are selected to take part in the research.

Using a survey approach in this instance raises an interesting question about whether or not this example of a survey should be seen as being a case study of schools in one local authority. This is further considered below. Even if you employ a survey approach in a large-scale social research project, then you will be making decisions about which cases are allocated to which groups. For example, your research may be a comparison of how members of different professions view their respective professional codes of conduct. You may intend to send a questionnaire to a large number of participants in a number of professions. Imagine you have decided to survey 420 participants in total, divided as in Table 3.3.

As you can see, you will have some choice about which participants are allocated to which groups. But in some respects, the choices are made for you, because of the criteria you have decided to use to group the participants. For example, all those participants who are in their first year of the profession and

Table 3.3   Allocation of participants in a survey

	Profession 1		Profession 2		Profession 3	
	Male	Female	Male	Female	Male	Female
In first year of profession	10	10	10	10	10	10
2–5 yrs' experience	15	15	15	15	15	15
6–19 yrs' experience	20	20	20	20	20	20
20–25 yrs' experience	15	15	15	15	15	15
Over 26 yrs' experience	10	10	10	10	10	10
N =	**70**	**70**	**70**	**70**	**70**	**70**
TOTAL =	**140**		**140**		**140**	

are female will be allocated to one particular group from a specific profession. In that sense, they are self-allocating.

Experiment

The researcher has the greatest level of control when using an experiment as part of their research. The cases in an experiment are created partly by the researcher and in a simple experiment there are two groups: the experimental group and the control group. In a true experiment, the researcher allocates cases to each group on a random basis. The groups are created to reflect the variables under investigation.

Table 3.4   Constituency of the different sub-groups in a calculations experiment

Experimental group 1		Experimental group 2		Control group	
Participants are told that the calculations will be difficult.		Participants are told that the calculations will be easy.		Participants are not told anything about the level of difficulty of the calculations.	
Group 1a	**Group 1b**	**Group 2a**	**Group 2b**	**Group 3a**	**Group 3b**
Participants have high level of mathematical ability.	Participants have low level of mathematical ability.	Participants have high level of mathematical ability.	Participants have low level of mathematical ability.	Participants have high level of mathematical ability.	Participants have low level of mathematical ability.

For example, you may be interested in motivation demonstrated by an ability to carry out mathematical calculations within a specified time. Your experiment, you have decided, will consist of three groups of students. Table 3.4 shows the constituency of the different groups.

How participants are allocated to each group is decided by the researcher, including the sub-groupings based on mathematical ability. It is highly unlikely that each group will have existed *as a group* before the experiment begins. However, the researcher's choice of allocating participants has been restricted due to the division of participants into high or low mathematical ability groupings.

Quasi experiment

Strictly speaking, most of the experimental studies that are carried out in educational and social research will be *field experiments* or *quasi-experiments*. These are experiments that don't quite meet the full conditions of a true experiment which are carried out in the human behaviour laboratory under carefully and consistently controlled conditions. They are carried out in the 'field', that is, in a naturalistic setting where the researcher has a reduced level of control over the above three criteria (and other characteristics of true experiments).

For example, imagine a school where a new approach to delivering the curriculum is being introduced in one of the year groups. Project work is being used as the basis of learning for three weeks during the first term of the new school year. It is to be a pilot and the school aims to find out how successful the new curriculum model is. The plan is for all pupils in one year group eventually to experience the new project-based curriculum. However, for the moment, as part of the pilot year, only half this year group will undertake the new project work. The rest of the year group will experience a normal curriculum based on a conventional timetable.

The researcher will randomly allocate pupils to the pilot and non-pilot curriculum groups, ensuring that there is an even spread of girls and boys across both groups. Although the researcher does not have full and total control over who the cases or participants are, they do have a degree of control over the decision to use two groups and to randomly allocate cases to those groups.

The researcher will also have control over which groups are subjected to the experimental condition (the pilot curriculum group) and which the control group (the conventionally timetabled group). *Relative* to using a case study or survey strategy, the level of control in an experimental approach, therefore, is much greater.

Please bear in mind, of course, that this is a hypothetical example. In reality, it may not be possible to divide a whole year group in a secondary school on a random basis. Pupils would probably be expected to remain in their usual classes, even for a cross-year project such as this one. This, therefore, would reduce the researcher's opportunity to employ random selection to allocate pupils to each of the two groups in the research.

Again, interestingly, this raises the question about how close this arrangement is to a survey? It has already been asked earlier about when a case study becomes a survey. The same question can be asked here: when does an experiment become a survey? We can also ask: when does an experiment become a case study approach to managing the data sources? Answers to these questions are discussed below but meanwhile you might want to consider what your own answers are to these questions?

Ecological validity

Ecological validity concerns the degree of naturalness of the research location and situation. In a study with high ecological validity:

> the situations in the research occur naturally. The intention here is to give accurate portrayals of the realities of social situations in their own terms, in their natural or conventional settings. (Cohen, Manion and Morrison, 2007: 110)

An important criterion, therefore, is the extent to which the research studies a natural and 'everyday' situation, without the researcher intervening to contrive, create or construct the research context.

Another way of looking at this is to consider the likelihood of any natural, everyday social activities coming to a standstill as the research is underway. The more the researcher intervenes thus resulting in the flow of activities being disrupted, the lower the ecological validity of the research. In other words, the more contrived the situation to enable the research to be carried out, usually the lower the ecological validity of the study.

A case study approach to data source management uses a naturally occurring situation, which is neither contrived nor constructed for the purposes of the research. The cases are naturally occurring and are studied in their real-life context. For example, observations of pupil behaviour can be carried out in a classroom. The case study in this instance is the group of pupils.

Creswell describes case study research as being carried out 'within a bounded system, a particular context or setting' (2007: 73), while Bassey describes case study as being an investigation 'of a singularity conducted in depth *in natural settings*' (1999: 47) (emphasis added). Yin (2003a; b) argues that using case study provides an opportunity to investigate an issue within its real-life context where what is being studied is not readily distinguishable from its context. If your case study is a group of pupils, as in the example above, then the pupils would be studied in their day-to-day lives within the school. As a result, the level of ecological validity would be relatively high. Activities are not disrupted nor is the situation contrived or created just for purposes of the research. In a survey, where ecological validity is lower than case study but higher than experiment, the research draws on naturally occurring cases but activities tend to be disrupted, for example when parents are asked to complete a questionnaire during a parents' evening at their children's school.

In a true experiment, with low ecological validity, the research location and situations are usually constructed, artificial and contrived. This might involve a number of participants undertaking a maths test, in a psychology laboratory, to determine the de-motivating/motivating effects of being told the tests are difficult.

Generalisability

Generalisability has already been mentioned in relation to the numbers of participants in research. Ecological validity can also be linked to issues of generalisability. Remember that, as Robson explains, 'Generalisability refers to the extent to which the findings of the enquiry are more generally applicable outside the specifics of the situation studied' (2002: 93).

If you want to apply your findings to a group outside of the research, then it follows that the closer the research situation is to the target of generalisation, then the more trustworthy will be the generalisation. This would suggest that if you use a case study as your data source management then you can feel confident that the generalisation will be trustworthy. However, usually, case study is seen to be problematic in allowing the researcher to generalise the findings outside of the study participants. One reason one is the small number of cases, as was outlined above. Another is the uniqueness of the situation usually associated with the case study.

Both the experiment and the survey tend to have medium to low ecological validity but have other characteristics that may – but only may – enable the researcher to generalise to other situations and groups outside of the research. These are covered in more detail in the next chapter about sampling procedures. You'll find that the idea of generalisability is still a contentious one and there are many issues that researchers disagree about.

▢ Summary 3.1

- There are three choices within data source management: case study, experiment and survey.
- Three main dimensions characterise your choice of data source management:

  - the number of cases
  - the degree of control the researcher has over which cases to allocate to which groups
  - the degree of naturalness, that is, the ecological validity of the groupings.

- Case study is characterised by a small number of cases, a low degree of researcher control and a high ecological validity.
- Experiment is normally seen to have a low to medium number of cases, a high level of researcher control and a low ecological validity.
- Survey usually has a large number of cases, a medium level of researcher control and a medium level of ecological validity.

Integrating data sources

Integrating the three different types of data sources can best be described using a three dimensional graph in the form of a circular illustration. Examples of the three different types of data source management can be plotted on the graph. Figure 3.1 shows three examples. Example A is located in the case study survey sector of the diagram. The example is characterised by:

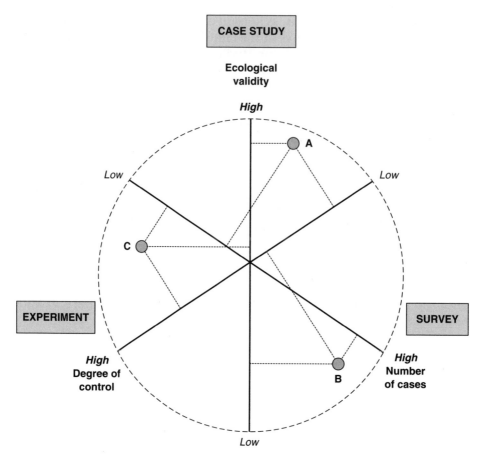

Figure 3.1   Integrating data sources

- a low to medium number of cases
- a low degree of control
- a high degree of ecological validity.

The researcher in example A will have a relatively low degree of control over the grouping of the cases, mainly because of the numbers involved. These are not high but, at the same time, there will be more than a *single* case. This particular case study might be a group of employees numbering, say, 12 to 15 in a medium-sized organisation. Carrying out research with such a group would take place in the work location. Consequently, there will be a relatively high degree of ecological validity associated with the study.

Point B in Figure 3.1 shows the characteristics of a survey-experiment approach to data source management, indicating:

- a relatively high number of cases
- a low/medium level of control
- a low level of ecological validity.

In this example, the researcher will work with a large number of participants or informants and have a limited control over those cases since the groups will already exist outside of the research study. There will be a relatively low level of ecological validity in the study since being asked to complete a questionnaire survey is hardly a natural situation in which to find yourself.

An example of such an arrangement might be a study involving students in a number of departments in a large university faculty. The groupings will already be relatively fixed with little opportunity for the researcher to intervene and allocate cases to different groups. However, there will be *some* opportunity to do this, since the groupings may focus on, say, the grades achieved in pre-university qualifications with which undergraduate students arrive at university.

The decision to use such categories and study such groupings will be the researcher's decision, hence the claim here for the researcher to hold some control over the data source management strategy. The ecological validity will be relatively low, however, since the research requires the intervention of the researcher with an associated disruption of normal day-to-day activities.

A third example will conclude this section about a number of selected issues associated with data source management. The location of point C in Figure 3.1 reflects:

- a relatively low number of cases
- a high degree of control
- a medium level of ecological validity.

This places the example in the experiment-case study sector of the diagram. This could involve a comparison of two small groups of participants to determine, for example, the incidence of RSI (repetitive strain injury) in laptop users compared to PC (personal computer) users. This particular research might be carried out in one department in a large organisation where some staff use laptops while other staff use PCs.

In this example, the two different groupings already exist, although the actual groups themselves do not exist *as groups*. They will be partly constituted for the purposes of the research, that is, they are not being completely artificially created for the research. In other words, the ecological validity or the naturalness of the groupings is neither high nor low, but at a medium level. The degree of control is reasonably high due to the amount of control that the researcher has over the decision to use the two groupings and the allocation of the participants to each group. The allocation of participants to the groups is not under the *complete* control of the researcher, however, since the contextual factors play an important part in the research.

The research is an example of a field experiment or a quasi-experiment. As Punch explains:

> The naturally occurring treatment groups are fairly clear cut, though not set up for research purposes. Therefore the experimental treatment is not controlled by the researcher, but the researcher has some control over when to measure outcome variables in relation to exposure to the independent variable. (2009: 219)

Table 3.5 When to use each approach to data source management

	Use a case study if you need to	Use a survey if you need to	Use experiment if you need to
Number of cases	Collect detailed, in-depth information from one participant or a small number of participants.	Collect general information or a wide breadth of information from a large number of participants.	Collect information from a small to medium-sized number of participants.
Ecological validity	Study participants in their own natural context with the minimum of disruption to ongoing activities in their everyday lives.	Study participants drawn from naturally occurring groups with some intervention and disruption to ongoing activities.	Construct the research situation to provide opportunities for manipulating the conditions under which participants operate.
Degree of control	Study one or a few participants in a naturally occurring group with no opportunity to manipulate allocation of participants to groups.	Have some control over the allocation of participants from naturally occurring groups to the research groupings.	Ensure you retain high level of control over which participants are allocated to which groups.

In this example, the independent variable is the use of a computer or a laptop.

When to use each approach to data source management

Table 3.5 provides an indication of when to use each approach to data source management.

You should bear in mind, of course, that the decisions in each of the cells in Table 3.5 will not be taken in isolation from each other. So that, for example, you would use an experiment if you needed to collect information from a small to medium-sized number of participants and needed to manipulate the variables utilising experimental and control groups where you are able to allocate participants to the particular groups.

Conclusion

This chapter has explained, in some detail, the criteria on which data source management is based. It has outlined the similarities and differences between case study, survey and experiment as the basis of data source management. It explained when to use case study, survey and experiment in research. In addition, there has also been the opportunity to apply the principles involved in data source management to the decisions you will make about your own intended research.

Once you have made a decision about which data source management strategy you will use in your research, then you will need to make one or more sampling decisions. Sampling decisions determine which particular cases to include in your research. The cases will be allocated to the groups resulting from your data source management decisions. The same process of making sampling decisions can be used for case studies, experiments and surveys. Chapter 4 will now explain this process more fully.

Reflections

1   Where on the case study/survey/experiment circle is your research located?
2   What are the implications of the location for the generalisability of your research?
3   What other methodological issues will the location create for your research?
4   How useful do you find the case study/survey/experiment circle for your research?
5   Are there any other dimensions that could be used in addition to ecological validity, number and degree of control for managing your data sources?

Associated reading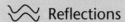

- Bassey, M. (1999) *Case Study Research in Educational Settings*. Buckingham: Open University Press.
- Blaxter, L., Hughes, C. and Tight, M. (2006) *How to Research* (3rd edn). Maidenhead: Open University Press. See Chapter 3, 'Thinking about methods'.
- Hammersley, M. (1992) *What's Wrong with Ethnography?* London: Routledge. See Chapter 11, 'So, what are case studies?'
- Muijs, D. (2004) *Doing Quantitative Research in Education*. London: SAGE. See Chapter 2, 'Experimental and quasi-experimental research'.
- Robson, C. (2002) *Real World Research* (2nd edn). Oxford: Blackwell. See Chapter 5, 'Fixed designs'.

Case selection: integrated sampling

This chapter will:

- identify different sampling procedures used to select participants for research
- explain the differences between probability and non-probability sampling
- indicate how to integrate sampling strategies with data source management
- enable you to apply integrated sampling decisions to your own intended research.

Introduction

Once you have made a decision about which data source management strategy is appropriate for your research, you will need to make one or more sampling decisions. Sampling decisions determine which particular cases to include in your research. The cases will be allocated to the groups resulting from your data source management strategy.

Making sampling decisions applies equally to case studies, experiments and surveys. If you use an integrated methodology for your research, it should come as no surprise that you can use a combination of different sampling procedures. At the same time, however, you should bear in mind that, as Blaikie points out: 'Sampling is frequently the weakest and least understood part of research designs' (2000: 197).

A sample is drawn from a larger group that is the focus of your research. The larger group is referred to as the population. Sometimes, the words 'sample' and 'population' conjure up images of large numbers of participants spread over vast geographical areas where the numbers involved are usually in the thousands. However, in small-scale research aimed at solving a particular problem or answering a specific question, the participants are often a relatively small group. They may be the pupils in a primary school or in a larger secondary school. Even in the latter, the population of pupils you are interested in may only be five or six hundred and sometimes even less.

It is not always necessary to take a sample from the population of study. In a small primary school consisting of only four teachers, it would hardly be problematic asking all four teachers to complete a questionnaire or take part in face-to-face interviews! Rather than take a sample you would undertake a census of the full population of four teachers in this instance. A census includes all cases in the population and provides information about the characteristics of the population as a whole.

A population can be divided into sampling units, which in turn consist of a collection of cases. For example, your research might be about how residents feel about living on a housing estate in a particular area. The sampling units might, therefore, be the houses and the cases would be the people living in the houses. As was mentioned in the previous chapter, not all research is about people so, in this instance, an alternative study might be about the physical state and disrepair of the housing stock on the estate. The population, therefore, would be all the houses on the estate. The sampling unit would be the streets and the cases the houses.

All the sampling units taken together should contain all the cases in the population. There should be no overlap between the units and none of the cases should be left out. This ensures there is no risk of counting a case more than once and every case is included in the research.

Sampling also applies to events. For example, you may be interested in acts of throwing litter in a shopping centre. You decide to observe the time of day when this occurs because you have been asked to decide when to deploy caretaking staff to pick up the litter. The interest here is not in the people who throw the litter but the *times during the day* this takes place.

Whatever the focus of your research, the main reason for selecting a sample from a population is that the population may be too large to include all cases or participants in the research. Including a full population would be resource-heavy, in terms of time and finances. In the litter example above, it would require an observer to note down all incidences of litter dropping in one location of the shopping centre. To observe all the time, every day of one week would require observers working in shifts from 8 a.m. in the morning to 10 p.m. in the evening every day for a full week.

In the desks example, mentioned previously on page 23, in a small school you would probably be able to find the time to look at every desk. But you would probably collect sufficient examples of graffiti for the purposes of your research without having to spend time looking at *every* desk. In other words, it is not always necessary to take a full census of the population: a sample will provide you with the information you need.

Summary 4.1

- Sampling strategy determines which cases or participants are included in your research.
- A census includes all cases in the population and provides information about the characteristics of the population as a whole.
- A population can be divided into a number of sampling units, which in turn consist of a collection of the cases.
- All the sampling units taken together should contain all the cases in the population with no overlap between the units and none of the cases left out.

Types of sampling

There are two types of sampling: a probability sample and a non-probability sample.

Probability sampling

A probability sample involves making a random selection of cases for your research. The aim of randomisation is to use a representative sample taken from a population. This will enable you to apply your findings to a group outside of your research. In other words, using a representative sample will enable you to generalise your findings from a sample to a wider population, by selecting a sample that is representative of the population to which you will generalise your findings. Bear in mind, of course, that it may not be the aim of your research to generalise your findings, but most small-scale research makes some attempt at doing this, even implicitly.

The four main probability sampling techniques are:

- simple random sampling
- systematic random sampling
- stratified random sampling
- cluster sampling.

Simple random sample

A simple random sample consists of choosing a number of cases at random from a larger group of cases. A random selection requires that each case has an equal and independent chance of being chosen. Beware, however, that arriving at a random sample is not as straightforward as it might appear. If the population you are interested in consists of, say, all of the 120 education officers employed by one particular local authority in England, then how will you take a random, representative sample of this population?

First of all, you will need to be able to identify all the officers and create a list of their names. This list is the *sampling frame* and like all sampling frames would contain the names of *all* the cases in the population under study. You would then number the names, from 1 through to 120, so that each name had a unique reference number.

If you now want to take a random sample of, say, 24 from the list, or from the sampling frame, one way would be to write each name or number on a piece of paper and put each piece in a container (or the proverbial hat!). You would then draw, at random, 24 pieces of paper with the names or numbers on. However, we live in the twenty-first century and there are now more sophisticated, electronic-based ways of generating a random sample for your research. A variety of random number generators can be found on the inter-net. You might like to look at the Research Randomizer. This is available without charge to students and researchers and can be accessed at: www.randomizer. org/form.htm.

Using the example of the local authority officers, information was input into the generator, as shown in Figure 4.1. The generator then produced the follow-ing 24 numbers: 1, 3, 18, 21, 22, 25, 28, 34, 39, 47, 54, 59, 61, 65, 66, 70, 71, 83, 85, 92, 98, 103, 104, 105. These numbers can then be used to identify the names of the 24 officers who would form the randomly selected sample.

Systematic random sampling

A systematic random sample involves selecting, say, every eighth or tenth name from a list. Randomisation would be built into the process by making the first name selected a random choice. In the above example, if the aim is to select a sample of 24 out of the total of 120, then you would have to select every fifth name from the list or sampling frame. This is quite elementary mathematics: 120 ÷ 24 = 5! However, you would still need to choose, at ran-dom, where your first choice on the list would be. In other words, which number will you start with on your numbered list of local authority officers? Using the random number generator on the Research Randomiser, you would input the following: sets of numbers = 1; numbers per set = 1; number range = 1 to 120 and each number to remain unique = Yes.

On this occasion, the Research Randomizer generated the number 75. This means the 75th name would be the starting point for the selection of a sample of 24 names, choosing every fifth name on the list. Once you reach the end of the list of numbers, you would then start again at the beginning, picking every fifth name until a sample of 24 had been selected.

Stratified random sample

Stratified random sampling involves dividing the population into different groups, that is, into different strata and then randomly selecting a sample of cases from each group or stratum. In the example of the local authority research above, you may be interested in gender differences. The local authority

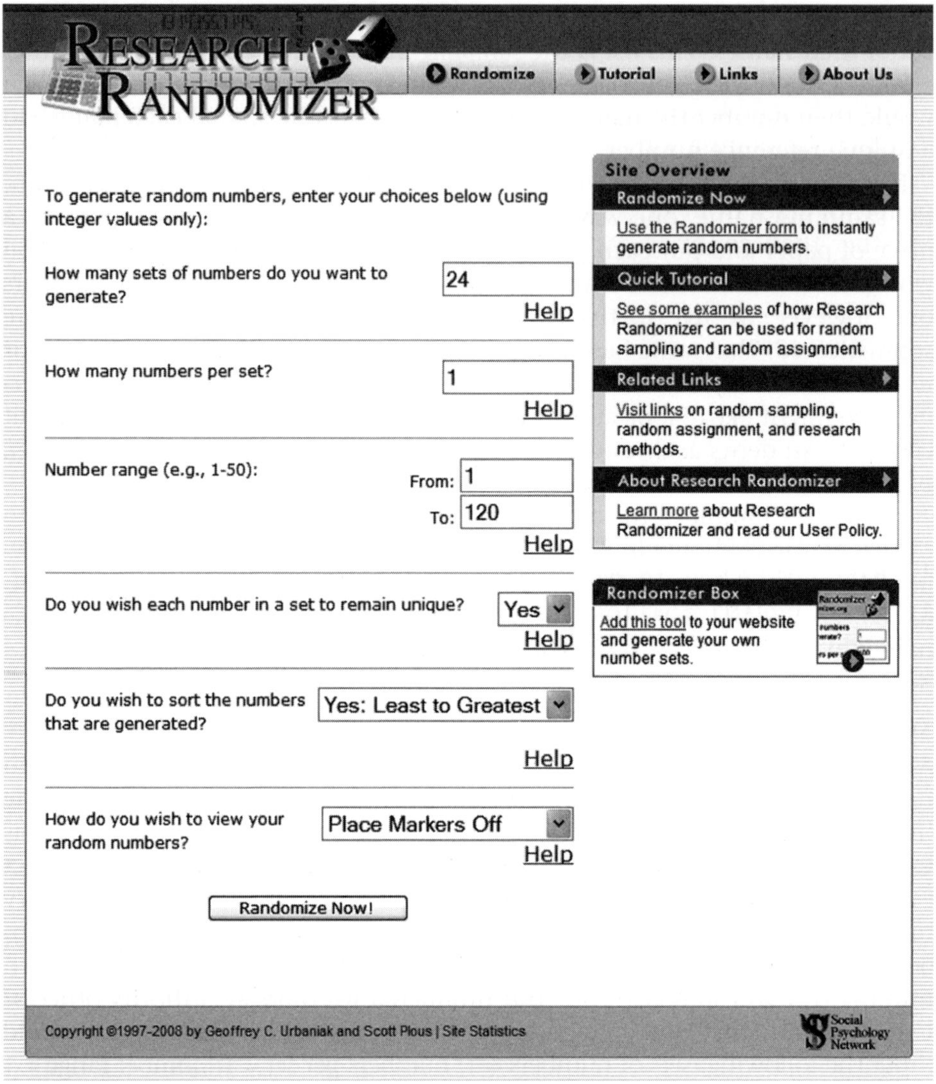

Figure 4.1   The Research Randomizer

officers would be divided into two groups: males and females. A random sample of participants would then be taken from each group.

Cluster sample
The above example of the local authority personnel has assumed so far that all the education officers are located nearby to each other, perhaps in one building. If the local authority offices were geographically dispersed across a wide area, then it would not be cost-effective to take a random sample of participants for the research. The cases selected would probably be dispersed

over the whole area of the authority. Therefore to meet with each officer would entail a lot of travelling, at some cost in both time and money. One solution would be to use *cluster sampling*.

A cluster sample requires you to select cases that are geographically close together. Randomisation can then include selecting, at random, a set number of clusters from the total number available and then randomly selecting a sample of cases from each cluster.

Rather than continue with the example of the local authority officers, a better illustration of cluster sampling would involve schools in the same local authority. Imagine you are carrying out research into the use of the self-evaluation form (SEF) that head teachers are now required to complete for their own school. Imagine your research involves examining SEFs from 24 schools. Assuming there are 400 primary schools in the local athourity and these are located in ten areas, with 40 schools in each area, the sampling strategy would require the following steps:

1 Four areas are randomly selected from ten.
2 There are 40 schools in each area.
3 Out of the 40 schools in each of the four selected areas, six schools are chosen at random.
4 The Research Randomizer indicates:

   - schools 8, 14, 16, 18, 25, 37 should be selected from area 1
   - schools 5, 9, 21, 25, 31, 34 should be selected from area 2
   - schools 9, 11, 19, 25, 29, 33 should be selected from area 3
   - schools 1, 12, 15, 16, 18, 20 should be selected from area 4

5 There are now 24 schools in the sample.

The golden rule about choosing a sample that is representative of the population is that whenever possible you should always build in randomisation. This distributes any built-in biases in the population across the sample and therefore aims to minimise errors in the cases selected. There is a complex statistical theory underlying this approach. If you are interested in pursuing this further then Coolican's (2004) and Oppenheim's (2000) publications will be worth looking at.

Summary 4.2

- There are two types of sampling procedure: probability and non-probability.
- A probability sample involves making a random selection of cases for your research.
- Randomisation enables you to choose a representative sample taken from a population.

(Continued)

(Continued)

- Using a representative sample will enable you to generalise your findings to a wider population.
- The four main probability sampling techniques are:

  – simple random sampling
  – systematic random sampling
  – stratified random sampling
  – cluster sampling.

Non-probability sampling

Sometimes selecting a random sample of participants will be inappropriate for the kind of research you are undertaking. For example, imagine that you are interested in evaluating the teaching strategies of the mathematics department in a particular secondary school. This school has an excellent reputation for supporting pupils and enabling them to attain high scores in national tests. You have chosen to research this school's maths department because of its particular characteristics, therefore, it has *not* been chosen at random. It has been chosen quite deliberately with a purpose in mind. This brings us to the second category of sampling strategies. You will have used a *non-probability sampling strategy* to make your selection.

In non-probability sampling, the choice of cases is not based on a ran-domised selection, but on criteria that provide a sample that meets a particu-lar need, depending on the aims of the research. Cohen, Manion and Morrison point out that:

> The selectivity which is built into a non-probability sample derives from the researcher targeting a particular group, in the full knowledge that it does not represent the wider population; it simply represents itself. (2007: 102)

In other words, non-probability sampling involves selecting cases that do not necessarily represent groups outside of the research. They are chosen because the researcher knows that they have information that will contribute directly to answering the research question. The four main non-probability choices are:

- purposive sampling
- convenience sampling
- quota sampling
- viral sampling.

Purposive sampling
The example above of investigating the high-achieving mathematics depart-ment is an example of using a purposive sampling strategy. As the word suggests,

there is a purpose to selecting the department. There would be no point in taking a random, representative sample of mathematics departments from a wider selection of schools. This would be a waste of time and effort since you would end up with some maths departments that are not high achieving.

Convenience sampling

A convenience sample allows access to participants who are conveniently located. Choosing such a sample requires little project management expertise. For example, you may be interested in the development of social identity in young children. You may have decided to carry out informal interviews with teachers and pupils. It's likely that you will decide to draw on a small number of participants, for a variety of reasons, including the amount of time the interviewing will take. How will you go about gaining access to pupils and teachers? Many researchers, including post-graduate students, use their already existing contacts with local schools since it is a *convenient* way of gaining access to a research site. In other words, this particular approach uses a *convenience sample*.

Quota sampling

Another non-probability sampling procedure is that of quota sampling. In the example above about social identity, imagine you have decided to carry out short interviews with pupils in one particular year group, aged nine and ten years old. There are around 55 pupils in this particular year group. You believe you could probably manage around 12 interviews, which will consist of open questions, collect narrative data and take around 10 or so minutes each. You could take a random sample but your sample would be unpredictable and may not result in an even spread of both genders. You would probably decide, therefore, to use a *quota sample*, of six girls and six boys.

Viral sampling

Viral sampling is traditionally referred to as snowball sampling. Blaikie points out that it is 'also known as network, chain, referral or reputational sampling' (2000: 205). However, the term viral sampling is preferred here, since we now live in a world that is permeated with communications technology where the idea of an electronic virus is well known. It is passed from one computer to the next, just as the researcher is passed from one participant to the next.

You may, of course, find it unpalatable to be compared to a virus but it works like this: your research may require you to interview students about, for example, excessive amounts of alcohol consumed in a normal week. It would be difficult to find a sampling frame that contained the details of such people. However, one way of contacting your informants would be via your friends or colleagues. This might involve the arduous task of combing the city bars and student union with requests for interviews from those who appeared to be drinking heavily.

At the end of your first interview you would ask your informant to put you in contact with anyone they knew who also drank excessive amounts of alcohol during the week. In this way, you would experience being passed from one informant to the next, much like a virus is passed from computer to computer!

Summary 4.3

- Non-probability sampling involves selecting cases that do not necessarily represent a wider population but have information that will contribute directly to answering the research question.
- The four main non-probability choices are:

  – purposive sampling
  – convenience sampling
  – quota sampling
  – viral sampling.

Integrating data source management with case selection

It is now time to integrate data source management with the case selection strategies that have been outlined above.

Imagine you have been asked to carry out research about the student accommodation at a university where you are either currently based or have been based in the past. The university is interested in finding out if improvements need to be made to ensure that residents have a pleasant and secure experience while living in university accommodation. There are 10 halls of residence, 85 student houses owned by the university and 40 houses leased from the commercial sector. Table 4.1 shows that, in any one year, there are 2,600 residential places available for students registered at the university.

Table 4.2 provides a brief insight into the possibilities of integrating both elements of the case selection component in the FraIM. Probability sampling can be combined with non-probability sampling procedures for each of the three different approaches to data source management.

The idea of integrated sampling is not a particularly new or innovative idea, however. It is automatically used in cluster sampling procedures to reduce the time and costs of conducting surveys and is referred to as multi-stage sampling (Gilbert, 2001). The important development here, though, is that it is legitimate to use different types of sampling with different approaches to data source management, depending on the research question and other components of the FraIM.

Conclusion

This chapter has explained that sampling strategy is integral to data source management and determines which cases or participants are included in your

Table 4.1   Number of places available in student residential accommodation

Category	Name of residence	Number of student places	City location
Halls of residence	Acorn Hall	195	North
	Beech Hall	131	North
	Bushy Hall	180	South
	Conker Hall	121	South
	The Elms	112	West
	The Firs	130	East
	Hawthorn Hall	120	East
	The Hollies	60	Central
	Maple Hall	122	Central
	Oak Tree	257	Central
University houses	85 houses	903	All areas
Private houses	40 houses	269	All areas
Total		**2,600**	

research. Both probability and non-probability sampling strategies can be applied to research conducted within the FraIM.

A probability sampling strategy involves making a random, representative selection of cases that enables you to generalise your findings from a sample to a wider population. A non-probability strategy is based on choosing a sample that has information that will contribute directly to answering the research question(s) and where the sample represents itself, rather than groups outside of the research.

This chapter has also argued that sampling decisions can be applied to case studies, experiments and surveys. It also outlined a number of examples that demonstrate that data source management can be integrated with the case selection strategy to ensure that the issues raised by the research question are addressed fully. The phrase 'integrated sampling' was introduced as an appropriate description of the process.

ᜑ Reflections

1 What type of sampling strategy will you use: probability or non-probability? Or both?
2 Do you intend to generalise your findings to groups outside of your research? What groups are they?
3 Which specific sample types will you use?
4 What will you do in order to select your sample?
5 What problems might you encounter when you are selecting your sample?
6 Will you have access to a sampling frame? If you don't have access to a sampling frame, what difficulties will this create for your research?

Table 4.2 Integrating data source management and case selection strategies in the FraIM

Survey	Experiment	Case study
1	**4**	**5**
Initially, a census of the population will be taken. All 2,600 students are invited to complete an online questionnaire. The aim would be to discover what residents believe to be the important factors that lead to a positive experience in residential living.	A group consisting of around 10% of residents living in university/private houses will be given a dedicated mobile phone, each with freephone access to a counselling support service.	An investigation will be undertaken of the experience of living in private accommodation. There have been a number of complaints about the poor service received from the university and the owners of the properties. Interviews will, therefore, be conducted with residents in a
	A second group of residents from halls of residence will be given the same facility, i.e:	sample of houses. The interviews will be relatively lengthy, in-depth, carried out in the houses and a large amount of detail will be collected.
2	**Houses group** **Halls group**	
A stratified sample is to be chosen, based on the three categories, or strata, of accommodation and then a proportionate sample will be selected as follows:	• Sample of • Sample of 60 residents (30 from 60 residents (6 from university housing each of the 10 halls and 30 from private of residence). housing).	Out of the 40 private houses used by the university, 8 (20%) will be selected. Initially a cluster sampling procedure will be employed. Geographical areas will be the north, central and south areas of the city. This is for convenience, including ease of access and travel from one area
1 Halls of residence: 550 respondents		to the next.
2 University houses: 350 respondents	• Quota sample of 30 • Quota sample of 30 males and 30 females. males and 30 females.	
3 Private houses: 100 respondents		
Respondents from each strata or category will then be chosen at random from a central sampling frame. They will be asked to complete a paper-based questionnaire about leisure interests.	Individual residents will be chosen from each category by random sampling.	The next stage will involve choosing, at random, two houses from the north area, four from the central and two from the south area.
3	After six months, the research will determine how often each group has contacted the counselling service and for what reasons.	Each house will be a case study aimed at revealing how the residents feel about the problems experienced in those areas. All residents of the houses selected will be interviewed.
A sample of 260 informants will be selected through systematic random sampling of all residents. Every 10th resident will be chosen from the central sampling frame. They will be interviewed by mobile or landline telephone to answer questions about their experience of security issues while in residence.		

Table 4.2 (Continued)

Survey	Experiment	Case study
6	**7**	**8**
An investigation will be carried out about the standard of food provided in all of the halls of residence. Two randomly selected students from each hall will be employed to carry out brief, structured interviews with a quota sample of 10 males and 10 females from their own hall of residence.	A stratified, purposive sample will be selected from all first-year undergraduate hall residents who have had a gap year prior to joining the university. The gap year residents will be divided into three groups 1 those who spent their time on a round the world trip 2 those who also went overseas but spent time on a specific volunteer project for more than six months 3 those who did not travel overseas but had a gap year in their own country. A fourth, comparison, group will consist of a random sample of first-year residents without gap year experience. A personality inventory will be used with all four groups. The aim will be to determine if there is any difference in personality types of students with different experiences. The results will be used to determine whether prior experience has any influence on gap year students' views of university accommodation. Outcomes of the research will contribute to future decisions about facilities for residents.	Five participants are to be chosen as case studies of students with disabilities who live in university halls of residence. The research will explore the experience of travel issues of getting to and from the university. The focus will be on perceptions of stress and its impact on life at university. The case studies will be based on purposive sampling of residents with disabilities. Additional residents will be recruited, through viral sampling, by asking participants to suggest others who they know have experienced difficulties in travelling to and from the university due to their disability.

Associated reading 📖

- Blaikie, N. (2000) *Designing Social Research*. Cambridge: Polity. See Chapter 6, 'Sources and selection of data'.
- Bryman, A. (2008) *Social Research Methods* (3rd edn). Oxford: Oxford University Press. See Chapter 7, 'Sampling'.
- Cohen, L., Manion, L. and Morrison, K. (2007) *Research Methods in Education* (6th edn). London: Routledge. See Chapter 4, 'Sampling'.
- Coolican, H. (2004) *Research Methods and Statistics in Psychology* (4th edn). London: Hodder Arnold. See Chapter 2, 'Measuring people: variables, samples and the qualitative critique'.
- Fogelman, K. (2002) 'Surveys and sampling', Chapter 6, in M. Coleman and A.R.J. Briggs (eds), *Research Methods in Educational Leadership*. London: SAGE.
- Oppenheim, A.N. (2000) *Questionnaire Design, Interviewing and Attitude Measurement*. London: Continuum.

5

Data collection: an overview

This chapter will:

- **describe the three different methods of data collection that are used within the FraIM**
- **explain the criteria which characterise the different methods of data collection**
- **provide examples of data collection strategies**
- **enable you to apply methods of data collection to your own research.**

Introduction

This chapter explains how the FraIM can be used to help you think about which methods of data collection to use in your research. By this stage, you will have determined what your research question is and its associated contextual factors; what data source management you will use and what your sampling strategy will be. It's now time to look at an overview of the methods you might use in order to collect the data.

There are three methods of data collection:

- carrying out observations
- asking questions
- undertaking artefact analysis.

If you have already undertaken some reading about research methods, then again, the above categories will seem a little unusual. However, Gomm, Hammersley and Foster (2000) refer to case study, experiment and survey as three major approaches to undertaking research, so this distinction is not a unique one. Indeed, once these are explained in some detail, then they will appear quite logical and sensible. They will also enable you to carry out research using an integrated methodology based on the FraIM. You'll find that this will encourage you to use a combination of methods of data collection, drawing on your chosen data source management to collect both numerical and narrative data.

A brief explanation of each of the three methods was provided in Chapter 2 and Figure 2.2 shows where they appear in the FraIM.

The three data collection methods can be characterised by two important criteria. These are:

- level of mediation
- degree of structure.

Level of mediation is a 'between-methods' characteristic and degree of structure can be described as a 'within-methods' characteristic. The former describes how a method of data collection can be distinguished from and compared to other methods. Its use is extrinsic to each method. On the other hand, degree of structure is a 'within-methods' characteristic that applies equally to each method of data collection. It describes how a method is internally differentiated, that is, in this case whether it is more structured or less structured. This intrinsic characteristic is used to evaluate each method on its own without any comparison with other methods.

Level of mediation

At one extreme, observational methods have a low level of mediation due to the researcher being relatively closer in time and space to what is being studied. Their position is *proximal* to the events being studied. At the other end of the continuum, artefact analysis has a higher level of mediation as a result of the researcher being relatively more distant from the phenomenon being investigated. Their position is *distal* to the events being studied. Asking questions lies between the two extremes.

For example, on day one of your data collection you may be observing a meeting between members of a project team. Imagine there are, say, eight people in the meeting. Let's assume you are interested in who tends to dominate the meeting and, as a result, appears to be more influential in the group. As you observe from an appropriate vantage point, your field notes record the interaction between the different team members. Your observations take place at the same time as the meeting takes place. This is represented by element A in Figure 5.1.

Then, imagine on the day after the meeting, day two, you carry out interviews with each of the eight participants. Your questions are about who they feel was more influential in steering the meeting and setting the direction of the discussion.

During the interviews, the researcher's experience of collecting data is not first-hand. It relies on the memory of the interviewees and their understanding and interpretation of what they remember happening the previous day. Your

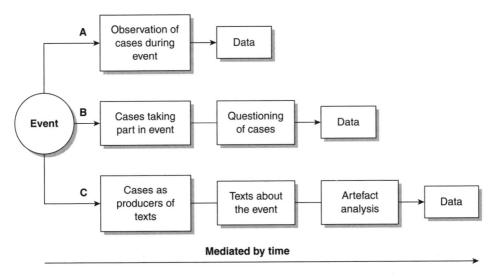

Figure 5.1   Time mediation

questioning, therefore, is mediated by time. This is represented by element B in Figure 5.1.

Imagine, also, that as part of your research each participant agrees to write a brief account of their views about what happened in the meeting. You have asked them to write about who they thought tended to dominate the meeting and set the direction of the discussion. Subsequently, you collect the written accounts and analyse the information, which is now using artefact analysis as a method of data collection. This is even more removed in time from the original event and the observations you carried out on day one. This is represented by element C in Figure 5.1.

In this example, the three methods of data collection are centred on one particular event. This need not necessarily be the case in all research. In addition, it is not a requirement that you carry out data collection using the three methods in sequence. Nor is it a requirement to use all three methods of data collection in the same research project. However, if you are using an integrated methodology in your research then it's likely that you will have already planned to use a combination of at least two different methods.

Figure 5.2 shows an illustration of three *different* research projects where each of the different methods is used.

In *Example D* the researcher collects data by carrying out direct observations of library users. The data collection is undertaken concurrently with the event being studied.

In *Example E*, the event is travelling to work. The researcher carries out interviews with the cases, a sample of the travelling public. The data collection is undertaken after the event has taken place. The cases are being questioned about their knowledge, understanding and feelings about their experience of travel.

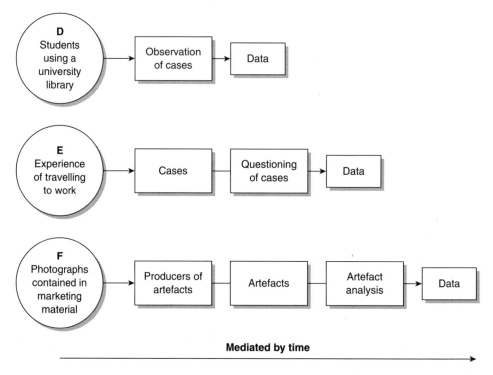

Figure 5.2   Three different research projects

Example F is about the use of photographs in below-the-line marketing material from a selection of SMEs (small to medium-sized enterprises). This includes promotional leaflets, booklets and sales letters. The 'event' is the phenomenon or issue the researcher is interested in researching. Let's say, in this instance, it is the gender of the people depicted in the photographs.

In example F, the process is slightly more complex. The first stage is the involvement of individuals who produce the texts. These individuals, however, are not the data sources. They *create* the data sources as a result of their activities. This leads to the next stage in the process: the artefacts, that is, the data sources or cases. Finally, analysis of the texts results in the generation and collection of the data.

An unfolding sequence

It can be seen therefore that, within each of the methods, a sequence unfolds to give each its particular characteristics and these are summarised below.

Observations

When undertaking observations, the process involves a relatively low level of mediation, entailing the following:

1   the event
2   direct observation of the cases or data sources
3   the data.

Asking questions

When asking questions, the process involves a higher level of mediation compared to observation. Arriving at the point where the data has been collected entails the following stages or elements:

1   the event
2   the involvement of the data sources or cases
3   the questioning of the data sources about the event
4   the data.

Artefact analysis

Finally, when artefact analysis is used as a method of data collection, the process involves a greater level of mediation compared to both observation and asking questions. Arriving at the point where the data are made available in the research entails the following stages or elements:

1   the event
2   the producer(s) of the artefact
3   the creation or production of the artefact or data sources
4   the analysis of the artefact
5   availability of the data.

Each method of data collection can be used independently on its own or integrated with each other. This latter is explained more fully in the next chapter.

Summary 5.1

- There are three methods of data collection: carrying out observations, asking questions and artefact analysis.
- The three data collection methods are differentiated by two criteria: level of mediation, a 'between-methods' characteristic; and degree of structure, a 'within-methods' characteristic.
- Level of mediation concerns how close in time and space the researcher is to the event being studied.
- Degree of structure concerns whether data is pre-structured or post-structured by using open or closed questions.
- Observation has a low level of mediation, artefact analysis a high level, and asking questions lies between the two.

Degree of structure

The 'within-methods' characteristic of data collection concerns the degree of structure that is a characteristic of each of the three methods. The degree of structure lies on a continuum. At one end the methods are highly structured and, at the other, they are less structured.

You may already have read about using degree of structure when carrying out research. For example, Blaikie (2000) and Bryman (2008) both use the idea of structure when categorising methods of data collection. Robson (2002: 270) writes about using fully structured, semi-structured and unstructured interviews. However, the term 'unstructured' is not used in research based on the FraIM. In fact, it is difficult to imagine what an unstructured approach to data collection would be like, since without structure, there would be no method at all!

In relation to observation, Opie points out that the term 'unstructured is used in some texts to reflect less structure, but neither case means that data collection proceeds with no aims or idea of what to observe' (2004: 122). Hopkins uses the phrase 'systematic classroom observation' (2002: 95) when referring to structured observation.

Degree of structure: asking questions

Table 5.1 indicates the characteristics that make up the degree of structure dimension for asking questions. Three of those characteristics are related to

Table 5.1   Degree of structure: asking questions

Low degree of structure ⟶		High degree of structure
Lower level of predictability over data *to be* collected	**Data**	Higher level of predictability over data *to be* collected
Lower level of pre-structuring of data	**Data**	Higher level of pre-structuring of data
Open questions	**Data**	Closed questions
Increased choice of participant response during data collection	**Participant**	Limited choice of participant response during data collection
Responses to questions are not predetermined	**Participant**	Responses to questions will be predetermined
Higher level of respondent control about how to respond to questions during data collection	**Participant**	Lower level of respondent control about how to respond to questions during data collection
Researcher has more choice over how the data are managed and analysed	**Researcher**	Researcher has less choice over how the data are managed and analysed
Lower level of researcher control during data collection	**Researcher**	Higher level of researcher control during data collection

the data, three to the part played by the participants and two to the role of the researcher in the research.

Low degree of structure

Data. When asking questions, the data are based on a relatively low degree of structure and the level of predictability over what data will be collected will be relatively low. This is because open questions will be used, leading to a limited pre-structuring of the data to be collected through open coding. This will be explained in more detail as the chapter progresses, but for the moment it is important to be aware that coding is 'the process of developing and using classifications for the answers to each question' (Oppenheim, 2000: 83). Open coding does not prescribe the categories or classifications used when the data are collected. The categories are usually developed during the data analysis stage, after the data have been collected. In other words, the data are not pre-coded, they are post-coded – after data collection.

Participant. As a result of the data collection employing open questions and, therefore, without the expectation of predetermined responses, participants will have a greater choice about how to respond and what to say or write. Thus, participants will have a higher level of control over the direction of the research and what information will be disclosed to the researcher.

Researcher. When asking questions has a low degree of structure, the researcher will have a relatively low level of control over what information is collected. This is due to the nature of open questions which gives participants control over what information is disclosed. However, the researcher will have more choice over how that data are managed and analysed, due to the lack of structure of the data collected. An example of using a relatively low degree of structure might look like the following question: what, in your view, can the government do to support employers to enable them to contribute to work-related education and learning, in your type of business? The item might form part of a questionnaire, to employers, about work-related learning for young people.

An open question such as this allows participants a greater choice about what to write. They therefore have more control over what information they will disclose. Conversely, the researcher will take a back seat, as it were, allowing the participant free rein in what views they want to express. In addition, the researcher will have more freedom in how the data are interpreted. This is because they will not be restricted by having to use predetermined categories constructed before the data are collected.

High degree of structure

Data. When the method has a relatively high degree of structure, there will be a greater predictability over what data will be collected. Closed questions will be used, allowing the data to be pre-structured before collection through closed coding. Closed coding sets and prescribes the categories or classifications used before the data are collected. In other words, the data are pre-coded before collection.

Participant. Using closed questions that invite predetermined responses, such as yes/no or agree/disagree, the participants will have a limited choice about how to respond to the questions and what to say or write. Thus, participants will have a relatively low level of control over what information will be disclosed to the researcher.

Researcher. Since the participant's choice of response is limited, due to the closed questions being asked, the researcher will have a relatively high level of control over what information is collected. It is often argued that when using this approach, we find out more about what the researcher thinks is important, rather than the participants! This is because the research is based very closely on the researcher's agenda. The participants have little choice but to follow that agenda. They have little opportunity to have *their* say about what *they* believe is important.

The researcher's choice of how the data will be analysed will be relatively restricted since the predetermined structuring of the data will, to a great extent, dictate the analysis.

Table 5.2 is an example of using a relatively high degree of structure when asking questions. It is part of an investigation of employers' attitudes to being involved in work-related education.

Table 5.2 Example using a relatively high degree of structure in asking questions

Question: What are your views about the current policy related to work-related education for young people?

Statement	Strongly agree	Agree	Unsure	Disagree	Strongly disagree
		Please circle one only for each statement			
1 I think 14 years of age is too early for young people to start learning for work.	1	2	3	4	5
2 I do not feel very happy about the proposed new system of post-16 qualifications based on a vocational diploma.	1	2	3	4	5
3 The new system of post-16 qualifications will help to meet the skills shortages in my industry.	1	2	3	4	5

As you can see, in Table 5.2 the researcher has determined the range of available responses, before the data collection starts. The data, therefore, have been pre-structured to fit the categories of strongly agree/agree/unsure/disagree/strongly disagree. The limits are set very precisely – there are no other replies allowed – and it is highly predictable what data will be collected.

When using the FraIM, you should find it relatively easy to integrate both structured and relatively less structured approaches to asking questions. At the very minimum, you should take the opportunity to include both closed and open questions in, for example, a questionnaire or interview schedule. Often, one or more open questions are included at the end of a questionnaire containing closed questions.

Summary 5.2

- Degree of structure concerns whether data are pre-structured or post-structured by using open or closed questions.
- A low degree of structure associated with asking questions is characterised by the following:

  – a lower level of predictability over the data to be collected
  – a lower level of 'pre-structuring' or pre-coding of data
  – open questions used during data collection
  – a higher level of respondent control about how to respond to questions
  – the researcher has more choice over what is recorded during data collection.

- A high degree of structure associated with asking questions is characterised by the following:

  – a higher level of predictability over data to be collected
  – a higher level of pre-structuring through the pre-coding of data
  – closed questions used during data collection
  – a lower level of respondent control about how to respond to questions
  – the researcher has less choice over what is recorded during data collection.

Degree of structure: observation and artefact analysis

There are some differences associated with the degree of structure in both observation and artefact analysis, compared to asking questions.

When being observed, the link between researcher and participant is more likely to be uni-directional: that is, the participants are not expected to intentionally respond to your observations. They are not expected to respond to you as a participant in the research, whereas when being asked questions, if they did not respond there would be no data!

Further, for most research that uses observation or artefact analysis, it would normally be unlikely and unnecessary for you to actively intervene in the

Table 5.3   Degree of structure: observations and artefact analysis

Low degree of structure	→ High degree of structure	
Lower level of predictability over data *to be* collected	**Data**	Higher level of predictability over data *to be* collected
Lower level of pre-structuring or pre-coding of data	**Data**	Higher level of pre-structuring or pre-coding of data
Open coding	**Data**	Closed coding
Researcher has more choice over what is recorded *during* data collection	**Researcher**	Researcher has less choice over what is recorded *during* data collection

participant's experience. That's not to say that the participant might not react to your presence. Potentially this can have an impact on the data collected. This is usually referred to as *reactivity* and this is covered in more detail in later chapters.

Table 5.3 indicates the characteristics that make up the dimension of degree of structure for carrying out observations and undertaking artefact analysis.

Low degree of structure

Data. When using a relatively low degree of structure, there will be less predictability over what data you will collect. This is because open coding will be used, leading to a limited pre-structuring of the data.

Researcher. With a low degree of structure, your research will be based on open coding of variables, with a minimum of pre-structuring of data. This will give you more choice over how you manage and analyse the data.

An example of using a relatively low degree of structure when undertaking observations is shown in Table 5.4. It is based on open coding and the

Table 5.4   Example using open coding during observational research

Observing non-verbal behaviour	
Participant A	**Participant B**
✍	✍

Schedule

1	**Size of advertisement**	*Please circle one number only*
a	Less than half page	1
b	Between half page and full page	2
c	Full page	③
d	More than full page	4
2	**Type of advertisement**	*Please circle one number only*
a	Product	①
b	Service	2
c	Product and service	3
3	**Type of product advertised**	*Please circle one number only*
a	Technology product	1
b	Non-technology product	②
c	Both technology and non-technology product	3

Figure 5.3   Coding schedule using a high degree of structure

researcher's task would be to record the non-verbal behaviour of the two participants, A and B, in conversation with each other.

It would be difficult to predict exactly what non-verbal behaviour would be exhibited during the conversation. However, it is not *completely* unpredictable, since the observer would probably record their observations as a narrative account of, for example, gestures, poses, eye contact and so on. The researcher would have quite a high degree of choice over what was observed and recorded due to the low level of pre-structuring of the data.

High degree of structure

In contrast, Figure 5.3 is an example of the use of a relatively high degree of structure when undertaking artefact analysis. It is part of a study of magazine advertisements. The research might involve looking through advertisements in a number of general weekly or monthly magazines (for example, *Good Housekeeping, Hello Magazine, Woman's Own*). A separate analysis would be undertaken for each advertisement using the coding schedule in Figure 5.3. The example is an analysis of a full page advertisement for a household product, which might be, say, a brand of washing detergent.

Data. The method used in this example has a relatively high degree of structure. Closed coding is being used, thus pre-structuring the data before collection. As a result, it is highly predictable what data will be collected.

Researcher. Due to the closed coding used, the researcher has less choice over what is recorded *during* data collection.

Summary 5.3

- A low degree of structure associated with observation and artefact analysis is characterised by the following:

  – a lower level of predictability over the data to be collected
  – a lower level of pre-structuring or pre-coding of data
  – open coding used during data collection
  – the researcher has more choice over what is recorded during data collection.

- A high degree of structure associated with observation and artefact analysis and is characterised by the following:

  – a higher level of predictability over data to be collected
  – a higher level of pre-structuring or pre-coding of data
  – closed coding used during data collection
  – the researcher has less choice over what is recorded during data collection.

Specific approaches associated with degree of structure

Table 5.5 indicates the choices open to you when deciding which approaches to use, based on degree of structure.

When using observation, you might consider applying a highly structured, closed coding schedule or a less structured, naturalistic approach using open coding.

Table 5.5   Data collection approaches based on degree of structure

Degree of structure	Observation	Asking questions	Artefact analysis
Highly structured	• Structured coding schedule	• Questionnaire • Interview schedule	• Content analysis
Less structured	• Naturalistic approach using a less structured coding schedule	• Questionnaire • Less structured interview	• Semiotic analysis • Discourse analysis

When asking questions, your strategy might draw on a structured questionnaire or an interview schedule aimed at collecting numerical data. A less structured approach might still use a questionnaire and interview schedule, with open questions inviting narrative responses.

Using artefact analysis would enable you to undertake a structured content analysis, perhaps similar to the one depicted in Figure 5.3. This could entail counting or measuring items in a chosen sample of artefacts. Alternatively, a less structured approach could involve a semiotic analysis or discourse analysis of the images or texts under study. These are dealt with in some detail in Chapters 8 and 9.

Finally, Table 5.6 provides examples of the different approaches to data collection, based on degree of structure. The use of different levels of mediation and degrees of structure raises different issues when carrying out research informed by an integrated methodology. For example, they create different potential sources of error and bias for the research. These issues will be explained and discussed in Chapters 6 to 9.

Table 5.6   Examples of different approaches to data collection based on degree of structure

	Observation	**Asking questions**	**Artefact analysis**
Highly structured	**Using a coding schedule** An observation schedule with categories based on closed coding. The researcher observes categories of behaviour that are predetermined. *Example: An investigation of pupil behaviour at break times that aims to record use of computers in an ICT area available for general use.*	**Using a questionnaire** A postal questionnaire that contains closed questions, with predetermined responses based on a five-item scale. *Example: Young people's views about the need for public transport in a rural area.*	**Using content analysis** A content analysis using closed coding that provides a count of the elements of interest in the text being analysed. *Example: A study of the number of times reference is made to issues about surveillance in a daily newspaper over a period of one month.*
Less structured	**Using naturalistic observation** A naturalistic approach to observing behaviour that is based on open coding and usually takes place in the observees' natural setting and location. *Example: A study of behaviour on public transport in a large city. This would involve the researcher travelling on public buses and making field notes about their observations. The notes would reflect the behaviour observed and might focus on, for example, aggressive and antisocial behaviour.*	**Using less structured interviewing** A less structured interview using open questions, often with the opportunity for the interviewer and interviewee to hold a conversation or a discussion about the topic of interest. *Example: A life history study of elderly residents in an inner-city area, drawing on memories of changes that have taken place in the area over the years.*	**Using semiotic analysis** An analysis of visual material using semiotics is undertaken, relying on the researcher drawing on their cultural understanding and awareness of signification systems. *Example: A study of the meanings associated with the portrayal of eco-tourism in advertisements in national Sunday newspapers.* **Using discourse analysis** Analyses of naturally occurring conversation and written texts are carried out using discourse analysis, which aims to critically indentify the way language is used in social relationships. *Example: Analysis of chat room text discussions, focusing on the use of abbreviated, idiosyncratic language.*

Conclusion

This chapter has looked briefly at methods of data collection: asking questions, observation and artefact analysis.

Observation includes covert or overt observing of behaviour. Asking questions can involve, for example, carrying out interviews or using self-completion questionnaires containing open-ended and/or closed questions. Textual analysis can involve the investigation of audio, visual and written materials.

Level of mediation differentiates 'between-methods' characteristics and degree of structure characterises 'within-methods' differences. The distinctions are important when you start to design your research and should be taken into account when planning which methods of data collection to use.

You can use one or more of the methods in your research. Your decision will be determined by your overall research aims and your research question. However, there is no 'requirement' to employ all three but you should now be more aware of the possibilities of taking a more integrated approach to your research than previously.

Chapters 6 to 9 look at the individual methods of data collection in more detail.

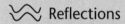 Reflections

1 Which methods of data collection will you use in your own research?
2 What degree of structure will your method(s) employ?
3 What problems might your choices create for undertaking your research?
4 Can you think of other ways to differentiate between the three methods?
5 How will you integrate the different methods of data collection in your own research? Draw a blank table like the one below and provide an entry for each of the six combination.

	Observation	Asking questions	Artefact analysis
Highly structured			
Less structured			

Associated reading 📖

Suggested reading for each of the three different methods of data collection is included in the following chapters that focus specifically on each method.

Observation

This chapter will:

- outline a number of selected issues associated with undertaking observational research
- take a wider view of observation compared to most other research methodology literature
- describe a useful approach to categorising observational methods
- provide examples to enable you to use observation in your own research.

Introduction

Your research question and the associated contextual factors will have enabled you to determine your approach to data source management and to decide on your sampling strategy. This next chapter covers the issues associated with using observation and is the first of four chapters that look specifically at which methods of data collection you might use.

In Chapter 5 it was explained that data collection methods are characterised by two important criteria: degree of structure and level of mediation. Degree of structure applies equally to each method of data collection and describes how a method is internally constituted, in this case on the dimension of more structured or less structured. Level of mediation is used to distinguish one method from another. Observation has a low level of mediation and, at the other end of the continuum, artefact analysis has a relatively high level of mediation, with asking questions falling between the two.

An observational method, therefore, can be described as being immediate or im-mediate. There is relatively less to mediate the impact or interpretation of the data collected. The prefix 'im' means 'not' or 'without' or 'lack of', as in *im*possible or *im*probable. In this context, it refers to the data collection process as being 'not mediated' or 'without mediation' by some form of media or by the passage of time. Observation generally takes place concurrently with the activities of the cases involved in the observed event. In other words, observation is very much about the here and now.

Using the FraIM

Compared to a more traditional approach to data collection, using the FraIM will enable you to take a wider perspective on carrying out observations. When you start to consider using observation in your research you will need to take into account the:

- sensory source of experience and empirical data in your research
- characteristics of different types of observer–participant interaction
- degree of structure and the related type of data.

Figure 6.1 brings these three dimensions together.

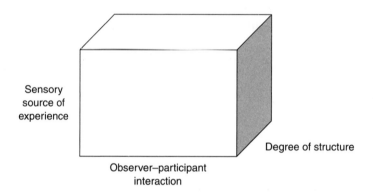

Figure 6.1   Three dimensions in undertaking observations

Different senses

A traditional view of the use of observation in research emphasises the activity of watching participants in order to collect data about their behaviour. However, an interesting point about observation is that it does not *just* involve collecting visual information. It also includes hearing, touching, smelling and tasting. Observation should, therefore, be considered a generic term that includes collecting empirical data via any or all of the five senses.

No doubt you may feel that this is a rather unusual perspective on the research process! However, we experience the world through our senses. We collect empirical information or data about the world through watching, hearing, touching, tasting and smelling objects and events. Usually, however,

I was shown around the home by two of the young residents. I saw how dilapidated the buildings were, and how dirty the rooms appeared to be. The washing facilities had not been cleaned for some time and must have posed a health threat. They had an unpleasant odour and one that I associated with my days in North Africa many years previously, where the level of poverty was almost unbearable to witness.

I heard the sound of children's voices: sometimes excited, sometimes quietly discursive. Adults too were talking and in the background I could hear the creaking of a metal gate that was hanging on to the gate post via worn and rusty hinges.

I drank coffee out of – thank goodness – clean cups and fortunately its taste was no different to any coffee I might have drunk in my own home or country. I was invited to stay and eat a sparse lunch, made from 'pap', a South African staple diet. I had tasted it before and wasn't keen to taste it again, so I declined the offer.

As I walked round the grounds of the home, I felt the unevenness of the earthen ground under my feet. I saw water seeping from a dripping stand pipe. The fetid smelling water mixed with the earth and the chicken and pig droppings, adding to the unpleasant odour that permeated the grounds of the home. The rough edges of the walls of the pig sty and the sharp metal fencing seemed intimidating and dangerous. One graze or scratch and who knows what lurking microbes would suddenly find themselves a new home.

Figure 6.2   Observations during an informal visit

it is only *watching* that is described in the methodological literature, although implicitly this can also involve hearing what is happening.

The five senses rely on *exteroception*, that is, they use receptors that receive stimuli external to the body. However, there are other senses that depend on *interoception*. These rely on sensory receptors that receive internal stimuli and include the vestibular sense, which is concerned with balance, and kinaesthesia, which is bodily movement and proprioception, that is, an awareness of the body's position in space and the detection of gravity (Gibson, 1986).

Although as pointed out above, most social and educational research uses auditory and visual data to inform the research process and its outcomes, it is possible to collect data using at least the other three exteroceptive senses. For example, imagine carrying out a research project in an organisation with which you are unfamiliar. Imagine, too, that the organisation is embedded in a culture that you are also unfamiliar with. This happened to me recently when I was visiting a small children's home in South Africa. It was an informal visit and I had not planned to carry out any systematic investigation of the organisation. However, I was very interested and curious about the people and the fact that the owners of the home I visited looked after a number of poor, orphaned children from the surrounding encampment. I took advantage of my visit to make a few mental notes about the home, with the intention of returning at a later date to undertake more systematic and planned 'observations'. Figure 6.2 provides a brief account of my 'observations'. As you can read, all five senses were employed to collect information about my experience during this informal opportunistic research incident.

Summary 6.1

- Observation uses methods that focus on the 'here and now' with relatively little mediation of the data collected.
- There are three dimensions to consider:

  - the sensory source of the empirical data collected
  - the characteristics of different types of interaction between observer and participant
  - the degree of structure and the related type of data.

- Exteroception involves the reception of sensory stimuli external to the body, that is, seeing, hearing, touching, smelling and tasting.
- Interoception involves reception of sensory stimuli that receive internal bodily stimuli, that is, proprioceptive, vestibular and kinaesthetic experience.

Types of observational research

In disciplines such as sociology and anthropology, there is a long tradition of observation, with researchers often using the term 'participant observation' to describe their activities. This is, however, not the only strategy that can be used during observation. A distinction is made between participant and non-participant observation. This is a basic description that is a good starting place if you are an inexperienced researcher. However, a more useful and sophisticated way of conceptualising the type of observation you might undertake is based on Junker's (1960) approach to fieldwork.

Table 6.1 is an adaptation of the approach that Junker writes about. The important criterion that distinguishes the kind of observation undertaken is not based on participation or non-participation, but is the degree of detachment or involvement experienced by the researcher. This reflects the *balance* of observer participation and non-participation in the activities that are being observed.

Full-observer

As a full-observer, the researcher will have minimal contact, or no contact at all, with the research participants. This would apply, for example, to psychology laboratory research where there would be limited interaction between the experimenter and participants. The observer located at this end of the continuum would take a relatively detached role. Indeed, the researcher may be undertaking observations covertly and so the participants would be unaware of being part of any research.

The main focus of the role would be that of a researcher. There would be no attempt at participating in any of the activities in which the participants were taking part. The observer would maintain a metaphorical distance from the participants involved in the activities and would aim to remain emotionally detached from the activities and the participants.

Table 6.1 Observer–participant interaction in observational research

	Full-observer	**Observer-as-participant**	**Participant-as-observer**	**Full-participant**
Role of the observer	Observer has minimal, if any, contact with the research participants.	Some interaction between observer and research participants.	Observer takes an established or more participatory role in the organisation's activities.	Observer uses their established role and position to conduct research or alternatively, secretly joins the organisation as a participating member.
Characteristics of observation	Covert observation in which participants are unaware of being observed.	Naturalistic setting where participants are aware of researcher and being observed.	Naturalistic setting in which member of organisation is carrying out research and participants are aware of being researched.	No one is aware of the participant acting as a researcher and therefore unaware that observations are being carried out.
Main focus of observer's role	Researcher carrying out observations.	<------------------------>		Participant acting as a researcher.
Emotional distance	Detached	<------------------------>		Involved

Source: Adapted from B.H. Junker (1960) *Field Work: An Introduction to the Social Sciences.* London: University of Chicago Press.

As well as a psychology laboratory, the setting might also be a naturalistic setting, that is, a real-life location where normal day-to-day activities are taking place.

Observer-as-participant

Further along the dimension, at the point when an observer starts to act as a participant, there would be more interaction with those being researched. It is likely that the observations would be carried out in a naturalistic setting and the participants would be aware that they were being observed. However, the observer would still remain relatively detached, with the main focus of their role being that of a researcher. They would maintain their metaphorical (and probably physical) distance from the participants involved in the activities.

Participant-as-observer

As a participant-as-observer, the researcher would take a more participatory role in the organisation's activities. This role might be an established one, for example, as an employee within the organisation. They would be taking part in the activities in which the participants were involved. The observations, therefore, would be carried out in a naturalistic setting and the participants would be aware that they were being observed. However, the main focus of the researcher's role would be that of a participant and they would, therefore, probably have already had substantial contact with other members of the organisation. As a result, it would be very difficult for such an observer to maintain an emotional distance from the issues under study or from the participants involved in the research.

Full-participant

As a full-participant, the researcher has the opportunity to use their established role and position in an organisation in order to undertake research without other members being aware that the research is being carried out. Alternatively, they may have secretly joined an organisation as a participating member in order to undertake the research.

A third possibility may include research that does not take place in an organisation, but in a particular social location. Well-known examples are a study of street gangs in an Italian slum in Boston, USA (Whyte, 1993) and the very unusual research carried out by Griffin (1977). In the latter, the researcher changed the colour of his skin to black (hence the title of the book, *Black Like Me*) and over a period time visited and lived in a black community in 1950s America. Other examples of this type of full-participant research are given in Chapter 13 and discussed in terms of the ethical issues raised.

In these examples, the researcher would play a full, participatory role in the ongoing activities. The observations, therefore, would be carried out in a naturalistic setting. The main focus of the researcher's role would be that of a participant. As a result, it would be very difficult for the observer to maintain an emotional distance from the research or the participants.

Examples of observational research

Table 6.2 provides brief suggested examples of research undertaken in each of the different categories.

☐ Summary 6.2

- Four observational strategies can be employed when undertaking research: full-observer, observer-as-participant, participant-as-observer, full-participant.
- The strategies are based on the role and activities of the observer in the research.
- There is a continuum from full-observer to full-participant based on the level of attachment/detachment of the observer, and the degree to which the observer participates in the activities being studied.

Table 6.2 Suggested examples of research categorised by observer–participant interaction

Full-observer	Observer-as-participant	Participant-as-observer	Full-participant
The researcher is sat at a table in a reception area of an organisation's main building noting the interactions between visitors and reception staff. Visitors and staff will be unaware that they are being observed.	The researcher visits a primary school and sits at the back of a classroom, noting down observations of teacher/pupil speech events. The researcher will have been introduced to the class along with an explanation that the researcher will be observing what happens in the classroom.	A member of the academic staff in a college of further education is collecting data for their research. They are interested in observing the senior leadership team during team meetings. The researcher is not a member of the team and does not usually attend the meetings. However, on a number of agreed occasions, the member of staff attends the meetings. All team members have given their permission for the observations of the meetings to be used for purposes of the research.	In another further education college in a different location, a member of the senior leadership team is collecting data for a research project. The research is about power relations between team members working at a senior level in organisations. They observe the senior leadership team during team meetings. In this example, the researcher is a member of the team and always attends the senior leadership team meetings. None of the other team members knows that the research is being carried out and that the team member is collecting data for their research project.

Advantages and disadvantages of different observer–participant interactions

There is a range of comparative advantages and disadvantages associated with the different strategies that an observer may employ during research. The advantages are outlined briefly in Table 6.3 and Table 6.4 lists the drawbacks.

The main advantage to being a full-observer is that the researcher will be unknown and will therefore be able to pass through situations and locations without having to become involved in the activities being undertaken. Since the research participants, as a result, will be unaware of the research, both procedural and personal reactivity will be reduced. When reactivity is present, it usually results in untypical behaviour (Bryman, 2008). Procedural reactivity

Table 6.3   Advantages associated with observer–participant interactions

	Full-observer	Observer-as-participant	Participant-as-observer	Full-participant
Reactivity	Reactivity is reduced or eliminated completely if the participants are unaware of being part of the research.	Reactivity will be reduced but may still be present.	Procedural reactivity will be reduced even further. Personal reactivity may also be reduced, depending on the researcher and the response of the participants to the researcher.	Procedural reactivity will be eliminated completely. Personal reactivity may be reduced, depending on the kind of activities undertaken by the researcher.
Knowledge of the research setting	As an 'outsider', the researcher will be fresh on the scene and will therefore not be influenced by past histories of participants.		As an 'insider', the researcher will have an increased insight and knowledge of the research situation. They will 'know their way around' and have an understanding of the culture of the organisation and the past and current political sensitivities.	
Access to participants	Access to public spaces may be easier due to covert observations being carried out.		Access will be relatively easy but will be partly dependent on which level of the hierarchy the researcher occupies and what already existing relationships are in place.	Informal access will be guaranteed since the observer is already a full-participant in the day-to-day activities of the organisation.
Managing the research location	Being an unknown researcher carrying out covert observation will reduce or eliminate the need to acknowledge knowing participants thereby reducing pressure to 'step out of' the researcher role.	There will be less pressure to step out of the researcher role and interact with participants on a personal level.	This will probably be relatively easier compared to the previous two categories of researcher. The researcher will be known and will know the research location, therefore will be familiar with spaces, accessibilities and availabilities.	

can occur when the research participants are aware of being studied and therefore behave differently, whereas personal reactivity occurs when the participants respond in a misleading manner to the researcher (Hammersley, 1992).

The main drawback of being a full-observer is that the researcher will be unfamiliar with the research setting and this may lead to difficulties of access and management of the observations.

Table 6.4 Drawbacks associated with observer–participant interactions

	Full-observer	Observer-as-participant	Participant-as-observer	Full-participant
Reactivity	If participants are aware of taking part in an experiment, procedural reactivity may impact on the research.	Both personal and procedural reactivity may take place.	Because the researcher is known, personal reactivity may impact on the research. The observations are not covert therefore procedural reactivity may impact on the research.	Personal reactivity may impact on the research as a result of the responses to the researcher as a person rather than as a researcher.
Knowledge of the research setting	As an 'outsider', the researcher will be unfamiliar with the research setting, therefore it will take more time to develop an understanding of the research setting.		As an 'insider', the researcher will already have a familiarity with the research setting and may therefore become too close to the participants. The researcher may lose a sense of detachment and become *too* involved, 'not seeing the wood from the trees'. This may be more of a risk in the role of full-participant.	
Access to participants	Access to participants will require a higher level of planning since access will have to be negotiated and maintained throughout the life of the data collection.		Access may be denied to areas of the organisation due to the sensitivity of the information to which the researcher might be exposed. This is partly dependent on the existing job position of the researcher.	Access might not be available since the researcher would not be able to explain the need for and justify the data collection since participants would be unaware of the research and the participant being a researcher/observer.
Managing the research location	Carrying out covert observation will not allow the researcher to rely on help and support from those in the research setting.	May be more time-consuming to achieve data collection due to the observer being unknown and unfamiliar with the setting.	Developing and playing the main role of a participant in the organisation's activities will be time-consuming. The experience could be psychologically stressful if there is a conflict between the roles of participant and researcher. These may well be exacerbated in the role of full-participant.	

The main advantage of the observer-as-participant role will be that the researcher will not be required to take part in any organisational activities that are taking place. The main drawback is similar to that of the full-observer, where the researcher is unfamiliar with the setting and location. The main advantage of being a participant-as-observer is that the researcher will already be familiar with the organisational context and location and will therefore not need to take time to develop an understanding of the setting.

The main drawback would be the potential conflict this will create in terms of the researcher's role, including the increased stress if that conflict is experienced as being insurmountable. The closer the observer is to the right hand side of the continuum the more pronounced will be these difficulties.

Summary 6.3

- Advantages and disadvantages of different observer–participant interactions are based on reactivity, knowledge of the research setting, access to participants and managing the research location.
- A higher degree of participation will lead to a higher level of reactivity.
- An 'insider' will have more knowledge of the research setting but may have to overcome a greater sense of involvement with the participants and location.
- A more participatory role will provide increased access to research participants.
- Managing the research location will be more demanding the higher the level of participation.

Ethical issues

It will, by now, have become clear to you that there are ethical issues associated with these different types of observation. If you are carrying out any kind of research without the participants being aware that they are the target of your observations, then you will need to consider whether or not it is ethically and morally acceptable to undertake such research. Chapters 12 and 13 deal in some detail with the ethical issues that are associated with observational research.

Degree of structure

So far, this chapter has looked at two of the important dimensions of undertaking observations: first, the sensory source of experience, and, second, observer–participant interaction. The third dimension is that of degree of structure. It was argued, in Chapter 5, that degree of structure is a major organising framework for any type of research, including research based on observation. So, just to recap: when you employ a relatively low degree of structure there will be a lower level of predictability over the data that will be collected. This is due to the lower level of 'pre-structuring' of the data as a

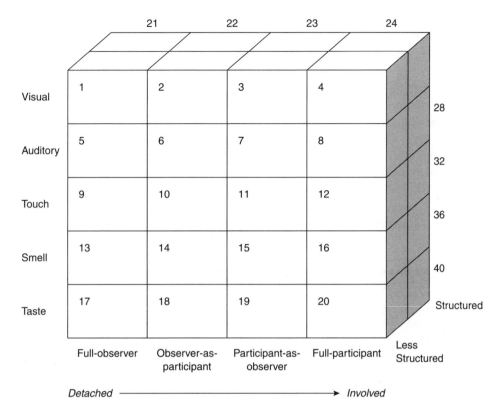

Figure 6.3 Undertaking observations

result of using open coding. However, at the same time, you will have more choice over what is recorded during data collection.

In contrast, if you use a relatively high degree of structure during the observational process, the data to be collected are *more* predictable. This is a consequence of the data being pre-structured as a result of the use of *closed* coding of the observations. Also, you will have *less* choice over what will be recorded during the collection of the data. These characteristics apply to all types of observation.

Integrating approaches

All three dimensions of observational research, sensory source of experience, observer–participant interaction and degree of structure, can now be brought together. This will demonstrate the increased level of choice that you will have when using the FraIM to carry out observational research. As you can see from Figure 6.3, there are now 40 possibilities open to you! This is a far cry from the usual way of conceptualising observational research as either participant or non-participant. Life as a researcher really is far more complicated and challenging than just having a choice of two approaches! In Figure 6.3 each cell is numbered from 1 to 40, but not all cells are visible in the illustration.

Table 6.5 provides a number of examples of how you might carry out research using different observational strategies. In these examples, the detached category of observer–participant interaction, that is, full-observer, has been chosen for illustrative purposes.

Imagine that your research is based on a comparison of selected jazz clubs in a city area. This requires you, of course, to spend some time visiting the clubs when they are open and in full swing. The research is exploratory and aims to provide a description of the differences between the clubs. Table 6.5

Table 6.5   Research based on utilising a full-observer strategy

	Degree of structure	
	Less-structured approach	**Structured approach**
Visual	**Cell 1** As you visit the first club of the evening, you make a note of the colours of the décor, the lighting and the type of tables and chairs you can see in the club. You might also note the appearance of the people who are seated and eating food or who are stood in the bar area. You find a not too crowded corner and start to write down your observations based on your impressions of the visual appearance of the club and the items in it.	**Cell 21** You arrive at the second club of the evening. You have already determined that you will use a more structured approach to your observations in this next club. You sit at a table and take out your observation schedule. This requires you to record: 1 the number of patrons sat at each of the tables in the main room of the club 2 the amount of time each person remains at the table before either leaving or moving to another table.
Auditory	**Cell 5** As you look around the club from your vantage point, you listen carefully to the conversations at the back of the main room. The evening hasn't really got started yet so the music is slow, quiet and in the background. The group consists of piano, double bass, drums and a bass saxophone. The music is unobtrusive and easy to listen to. Your data collection consists of writing down your observations based on your impressions of the noises, sounds and music you can hear in the club.	**Cell 26** You have set yourself two tasks associated with observing based on your auditory experiences. The first involves calculating the amount of time that music is played in the club. Your observations record the amount of time: 1 the group plays live music 2 the club plays pre-recorded music over the PA system 3 no music is played. The second task is to use a rating scale to assess the noise level in each club you visit. The scale is calibrated on a 10 point dimension from 'comfortable' to 'painful'. You carry out the assessment every 10 minutes over a period of two hours, giving you 12 sampling points for each club you visit.

Table 6.5 (Continued)

	Degree of structure	
	Less-structured approach	**Structured approach**
Touch	**Cell 9** After not too long, your attention turns to the chairs people are sitting on. They're made of cold, hard white plastic. Maybe the owners thought they would look trendy? They feel unfriendly, however, unwelcoming and hard to the touch. The seat has rough edges and cold, metallic legs are splayed out underneath the seat and take up more space than they should. You decide to find out if other visitors to the clubs feel the same way. Your data collection consists of asking questions through interviewing the patrons about their views of the material used in the clubs, including the furniture, the floor coverings and the bar.	**Cell 29** To carry out observations based on the sense of touch, you have decided to take a relatively straightforward approach and record the temperature of the clubs you visit. You're able to do this using a simple thermometer. Your approach involves noting the air temperature in one location of the club every 10 minutes over a period of two hours. As with the auditory observations, this will give you 12 sampling points for each club you visit.
Smell	**Cell 13** After a few minutes, a waiter approaches you and you order a drink. You can already smell the food. There is a predominance of the smell of garlic in the impressions you gather from the aromas wafting from the noisily opening and closing door of the kitchen area. The olfactory impressions are all quickly noted, as you decide you will have a bite to eat before you leave this first club. You therefore order cheese nibbles and a small glass of orange juice. Your data collection consists of noting down your impressions of the smells and aromas of the club.	**Cell 33** You decide to carry out a direct investigation into the aromatic characteristics of the different clubs that are part of your research. From your observations, you rate on a five-point scale how noticeable or how pleasant or interesting the aromas of the clubs appear to be.
Taste	**Cell 17** You decide the cheese nibbles are delicious and you nearly give in to the temptation of ordering more. However, you carry on making notes about the impressions you have received so far about the club and now focus on the tastes of the food and drink. Your data collection consists of noting your impressions of the tastes you experience while at the club.	**Cell 37** You carry out a direct investigation into how appetising the food is, using a seven-point rating scale. The scale ranges from extremely appetising to extremely unappetising for each of the items you select from the menu. The research will enable you to compare the food that is served in each of the clubs you visit.

briefly outlines the approaches that you might take as you travel or, perhaps after a few visits in the same evening, stagger around the different jazz clubs. Initially, any research project would need to negotiate and agree access to the venues. Let's assume you achieve this prior to the data collection, so the club managers/owners know you will be on their premises and are supportive of your research. The cell numbers refer to the cells in Figure 6.3. As you can see from the examples, the full range of the senses can be used as the basis for collecting both narrative and numerical data.

 Summary 6.4

- There are a number of ethical issues associated with the different observer roles, especially where covert research is involved.
- You will need to take into account the degree of structure of data collection covered in Chapter 5 when carrying out observational research.
- An integrated methodology results in 40 potential different observation strategies based on the five senses, the continuum of different roles and the degree of structure in data collection.

Conclusion

As a result of reading through this chapter, you'll now be aware that observation is far more complex than most methodology textbooks would seem to suggest. This is because observation is about more than simply *looking at* what participants are doing. It's even *more than what they say*, when they are doing it, whatever 'it' might be!

Observation includes collecting data through using different sensory experiences. Obviously, the two main senses are sight and sound. It is not always possible, or indeed desirable, to draw on data collected through the other sensory experiences of touching, smelling and tasting. However, once you become aware of the complexities of observational research then you are provided with a wider choice of how you might go about collecting your data.

It is interesting that data collection using the five different senses raises a number of intriguing issues about the primacy of using sight and sound in developing and maintaining an understanding of the world around us. The poorly developed and under-used data collection techniques based on the other sensory areas of touch, smell and taste are mirrored by the inadequacies of these senses in keeping us fully informed of what is happening in our environment. Yes, we do use touch, taste and smell but we usually rely on sight and sound to maintain a *continuous* contact with our surrounding world. The smells and tastes of that world impinge on us only at certain times and we use touch relatively infrequently to collect information about our surroundings. Methods of data generation, collection and analysis are under-developed in these lesser used sensory areas.

Further, the ideas and approaches to carrying out observational research outlined in this chapter have not included the use of strategies based on the interoceptive approaches of proprioceptive, vestibular and kinaesthetic sensory perception. Such data collection approaches are even more under-developed!

Using the FraIM on which to base your research provides opportunities to develop your understanding of how the full range of senses might be employed in research activities. As always, you are invited to jettison a traditional and blinkered way of carrying out these activities and think through how you might integrate the different types of observations. Figure 6.3 makes it clear that you have the potential to select from a total of 40 types of observational research! This is without drawing on interoceptive sense data.

The question now is: how many observational methods will you be using in *your* research?

⌇⌇ Reflections

1   If you intend to base your data collection on observational methods, what type of observation will you use?
2   What are the advantages of the types(s) of observation you will employ?
3   How will you integrate the different observation strategies?
4   What role(s) will you, as the researcher, play?
5   What problems do you anticipate during the observations?
6   Which of the 40 cells from Figure 6.3 will your research fall into?

Associated reading 📖

* Hammersley, M. and Atkinson, P. (1995) *Ethnography: Principles in Practice.* London: Routledge.
* Hume, L. and Mulcock, J. (2004) *Anthropologists in the Field: Cases in Participant Observation.* New York: Columbia University Press.
* Moyles, J. (2002) 'Observation as a research tool', Chapter 11 in M. Coleman and A.R.J. Briggs (eds), *Research Methods in Educational Leadership.* London: SAGE.
* Palaiologu, I. (2008) *Childhood Observation.* Exeter: Learning Matters.
* Pellegrini, A.D. (2004) *Observing Children in their Natural Worlds: A Methodological Primer* (2nd edn). Mahwah, NJ: Lawrence Erlbaum.
* Sanger, J. (1996) *The Compleat Observer? A Field Research Guide to Observation.* London: Falmer Press.
* Wragg, E.C. (1999) *An Introduction to Classroom Observation* (2nd edn). London: Routledge.

Asking questions

This chapter will:

- show how asking questions is based on using written and spoken questions employing face-to-face, paper and electronic media
- demonstrate how to integrate different approaches to asking questions as a method of data collection
- provide examples that will enable you to make a start in using asking questions to collect data in your own research.

Introduction

This chapter looks at the procedures and processes involved in collecting data through the second of the data collection methods: asking questions. Chapter 5 pointed out that this can involve carrying out interviews or using self-completion questionnaires. This suggests that asking questions of your informants or participants is quite a straightforward process. However, this chapter takes this process further and shows that there is more to asking questions than Chapter 5 may have led you to believe!

First of all, questions can be either written or spoken. They can also be delivered through different media, as shown in Table 7.1.

Written questions

Table 7.1 shows that if you intend to use written questions then you can use a range of different media. These media are often used together and, as you'll discover after reading this chapter, can be integrated in a number of different ways.

Face-to-face

Combining written questions or a written test with a face-to-face medium will involve handing out the written material to participants in the same room or locality as the researcher.

Table 7.1 Asking questions using different media

	Medium		
	Face-to-face	**Paper**	**Electronic**
Written	• In-situ questionnaire • Written test	• Postal questionnaire	• Online questionnaire • Email/fax, • Chat room • Mobile/cellphone text messaging
Spoken	• One-to-one interview • Group interview • Focus group	• Interview schedule used during one-to-one interview • Group interview and focus group meeting	• Video-conferencing • Telephone • Mobile/cellphone

Paper

Questions posed via a written questionnaire are regularly used during research. Indeed, a questionnaire is often the only means used to collect data. You will probably be anticipating using a survey if you intend to contact a large sample of respondents (Fink and Kosecoff, 1998) as was outlined in Chapter 3 about data source management.

Electronic

Written questions that employ electronic media include web-based questionnaires, email, chat rooms and mobile phones. Because the use of electronic media is relatively new, the rest of this section looks specifically at this approach to data collection.

Email

Electronic media can be used for distributing a questionnaire that, in the past, would have found its way to respondents via the postal system. Now, of course, there is the ubiquitous email. One of the major difficulties with using email and indeed any electronic, web-based strategy to distribute questionnaires is the demands of compiling a sampling frame. You'll remember from Chapter 4 that a sampling frame is a physical source containing contact information for all the cases. Usually, with both email and web-based approaches, the sampling frame is simply a list of names and email addresses. Getting access to such a list isn't always easy.

If your research is located in your own organisation, then you may have access to the full list of email addresses for people in the organisation. If you want to contact groups outside of your organisation, then you will need to use an alternative source of information. But don't despair: there are sources of names, postal and email addresses and, in some cases, even mobile phone numbers to which you can get access. This information can be accessed via what is referred to as a *list broker*. A list broker is an organisation that acts as an intermediary between the owner of a list of names and contact details and anyone who wants to use the list.

One list broker you might want to look at that can be accessed via the internet is www.listbroker.com. This particular organisation would be able to supply you with email and postal addresses for a variety of potential respondents ranging from parents, farmers and medical professionals to health and safety workers and even students registered on degree programmes in the UK.

Information from any list broker is normally used by commercial businesses for marketing purposes. One example of a list owner which you probably won't be familiar with, but one that may contain information about your own contact details if you are a student, is Campus Media (www.campusgroup. co.uk). It is owned by MAMA Group Plc, which was founded in 2002, and is a public company working in the music and media businesses. The names on this list are collected at the beginning of the university year, when students activate their NUS (National Union of Students) cards online. According to their website, the list contains over 800,000 names and contact details, including a full list of email addresses and SMS (short message service) details for over a quarter of a million students.

If you are a UK student, then no doubt you will already have received mailshots and emails from companies and organisations trying to sell you products or goods. You might have wondered where they got your details from. Now you know!

Web-based questionnaires

One method of collecting data that is being used increasingly in social and educational research is the use of online, web-based products. These can reach a large sample of respondents. They are relatively cheap and very quick to administer. Often, an organisation's VLE (virtual learning environment) incorporates an electronic survey function.

In addition, opportunities are now available that enable you to design and distribute online surveys using electronic questionnaires. Generally speaking, these are easy to use but can be costly. A search of Google using the term 'electronic surveys' reveals a wealth of internet sites. One company, Key Survey (www.keysurvey.co.uk), at the time of writing, allows a 30-day free trial. This enables users to try out the web-based system before purchasing a subscription to the full software package and internet tools. For this you get to create and automatically distribute your survey via email. The company's web pages collect the response data via the web pages. It will even automatically produce a report of the analysis of the information that your respondents provide online.

Another useful website is Survey Monkey (www.surveymonkey.com). A basic version of the web-based survey software is available free of charge, allowing 10 questions per survey and 100 responses per month. There is an additional charge for an upgraded version which gives you more powerful functions.

This whole area is relatively new although research using web-based approaches is increasing. For example, Shannon et al.'s article is worth a read. These authors asked 62 experienced survey researchers from the American Educational Research Association about using electronic surveys. The study is published in *Practical Assessment, Research and Evaluation*, a peer-reviewed electronic journal with open access via the internet. The respondents were asked 'to describe conditions under which the use of email or web-based surveys would be most appropriate, define appropriate samples, identify the major weaknesses, and offer recommendations for other researchers that plan to use email or the Internet to assist their survey research projects' (Shannon et al., 2002: 1). The findings showed that using electronic surveys can reduce postage and phone costs and provide an opportunity to use electronic mail for pre-notifying potential respondents and for follow-up purposes.

Chat room

Another way of asking questions via electronic media is by using chat rooms. Rhodes, in an article reporting a study of a chat room based HIV prevention intervention for gay men, provides a clear explanation of what a chat room is and how it is used by 'chatters':

> A chat room is a channel of synchronous dialogue among computer users who are connected through a network of computers ... Chatters can type messages on their computers that are transferred almost instantaneously by the server to the other chatters within the chat room. Thus, chatters are able to talk to each other in 'real time'. (2004: 316)

Not surprisingly, this approach to data collection has not received extensive use, at least not yet. One study, however, that exploited young people's interest in the internet and chat rooms was carried out by Woodruff et al. (2007). The research investigated the effectiveness of a stop smoking programme for school students. One group in the study took part in an internet-based, virtual reality world combined with interviewing and group discussion via a chat room using text. A comparison group completed online surveys. This approach to asking questions appeared to be well received by the school students taking part in the research.

Most VLEs (virtual learning environments) contain synchronous chat room facilities. This allows participants to type in text and 'talk' to other participants in real time. One of the disadvantages of carrying out interviews in some chat rooms is that anyone registered on the site can read the messages that are sent between the two participants. Some chat rooms, however, have the facility for members to take part in private conversations with each other. This would be more appropriate for carrying out one-to-one interviews, especially if the focus of the research was a personal, sensitive or contentious issue.

Mobile or cellphone

Another as yet under-used method of asking questions to collect data is via mobile or cellular phone messaging or texting. Again, it is not too surprising that this approach has not been used extensively, due to the relatively new application of this particular technology to carrying out research.

As with using email for contacting respondents, the main difficulty with expecting to use SMS via wireless cellular telephony is the access to a sampling frame. It *is* possible, via a list broker, but there would be no guarantee you would receive many replies to your SMS texts. In addition, your question(s) would be restricted to using only a few characters and it would be expensive for the amount of information you would be able to send and collect.

Bryman discusses a number of issues associated with the use of e-research and his chapter, 'E-research: using the Internet as object and method of data collection' (2008: 466–88), is highly accessible and well worth reading. You might also want to look at Gillham's (2005) publication which includes chapters on telephone, video and email interviewing.

 Summary 7.1

- Questions can be either written or spoken.
- Written questions can be delivered using face-to-face, paper-based or electronic media.
- Written questions that use electronic media include web-based online questionnaires, email, chat rooms and mobile phones.
- Compiling a sampling frame can be problematic generally, but especially when using electronic media.
- A list broker can very often provide names, postal addresses, email addresses and mobile phone numbers.

Finally, in this section, the following provides a brief description of the characteristics of using written questions in each of the three different media.

Using face-to-face media can be a very convenient and manageable method of delivering a written questionnaire if a full sample of participants can be gathered together in the same location at same time, such as a class of pupils. This also applies to a written test given to participants to assess or evaluate their abilities. However, participants may be aware of taking part in a research project and so reactivity may occur to influence their responses.

When you use paper media, a large number of respondents can be contacted, assuming you have access to a reliable sampling frame. However, as the researcher, you have no control over the conditions under which the questions are answered. In fact, you do not even have control over who answers the questions! In addition, the questions may be completed in any order, although this may not be problematic. A relatively high degree of literacy is usually needed to complete a written questionnaire. The final point to note here is that the response rate for a postal questionnaire is notoriously low. If you receive a 10 per cent return, then you can be pleased!

It may be quite a challenge to compile a sampling frame when you use electronic media. If you do have a sampling frame, then a relatively large number of respondents can be emailed and thus this can be a relatively cheap method of distribution. Using SMS to contact respondents is under-used and may turn out to be ineffective due to the length of the message you can use. However, in contrast to using paper media, you would be able to control the order of the questions answered when using a web-based electronic question-naire, although this does not apply to questionnaires that are emailed to respondents.

Spoken questions

Spoken questions can be asked when the researcher is *face-to-face* in one-to-one interviews, group interviews and focus groups. *Paper-based* spoken ques-tions can also be used in the same situations. *Electronic* media can employ video-conferencing, telephone and wireless cellular/mobile phones.

It has already been mentioned that not only can you use these methods together but they are often integrated to allow for the maximum benefit for the data collection process. For example, you might use paper-based questions using video-conferencing. One-to-one and group interviews can be under-taken while using a telephone or taking part in a video-conferencing event. In other words, there can at times be a natural integration of both written and spoken questions using different media.

There is a wealth of published material about interviewing and suggestions for associated reading are included at the end of this chapter. As you would expect, there is not quite so much information on the bookshelves or in cyber space about the use of electronic media, although this appears to be growing.

You may already be familiar with a number of different technologies for using video-conferencing. One of those is Skype. This is a commercial system that is downloaded from the internet. Once installed on your computer Skype to Skype calls are free of charge. Calls are made over the internet. You can also use a webcam. This means not only can you talk to the person on the other end of the connection but you can also see them at the same time in fully animated colour, action and speech. Additional software can also be used to enable you to record the conversation or interview. Obviously, as with any other situation in which you record what participants say, there are ethical issues that will need to be addressed.

The following provides a brief summary of the characteristics of using spoken questions in each of the three different media.

When using a face-to-face medium, one-to-one or group interviews can be carried out. You can offer a personal presence during the data collection which will allow you some control over the conditions under which the questions are asked.

Using paper-based questions, a questionnaire can be read to the respondents or an interview guide can structure an interview and give it direction. In addition, the questions can be sent to respondents before the interview takes place, so they have time to think through their answers and are prepared when you meet them.

When using electronic media, you can conduct one-to-one or group interviews via video-conferencing or telephone and therefore you can offer a *virtual* presence during the data collection.

Whatever the media, when using spoken questions, you will have control over the *manner* in which the questions are asked and in what *order*. Both closed and open questions can be asked and you will be able to clarify the questions or prompt the interviewees if they are unsure of the meaning of any of the questions or items. However, you should bear in mind that the participants will be aware of taking part in a research project and so reactivity may influence their responses.

Integration of approaches to asking questions

It will be clear by now that when you use an integrated methodology for asking questions, not only is there a choice of approaches, but it is actually quite difficult to avoid using more than one approach! Even a relatively straightforward face-to-face interview can involve using a paper-based interview schedule or asking the questions via a web-based electronic system. In addition, a written, paper-based questionnaire can be distributed electronically via email or as a fax.

As you plan and prepare your approach to asking questions as a method of data collection, do be aware of integrating the different approaches. Bear in mind that the focus should be on a respondent-centred strategy. It is important therefore to think through how you might want to present the questions to your respondents.

Summary 7.2

- Face-to-face spoken questions can be used in one-to-one interviews, group interviews and focus groups.
- Paper-based spoken questions can also be used in one-to-one interviews, group interviews and focus groups.
- Using electronic media for spoken questions can employ video-conferencing, telephone and wireless cellular/mobile phones.
- Integrating approaches to asking questions is based on a respondent-centred strategy.
- An integrated approach using both written and spoken questions uses a combination of different media.

Degree of structure

You will know by now that degree of structure is an important characteristic of data collection.

Using the FraIM, it is worth considering building into your research closed and open questions that collect both narrative and numerical data. Sometimes, researchers use closed questions as the main approach. They then include open questions to give respondents an opportunity to write about their own views. On other occasions, exploratory research may use open questions to gain an understanding of an issue and then follow up with closed questions to test that understanding or focus on the issue in more detail and depth (Creswell and Plano Clark, 2007).

An alternative approach to asking both closed and open questions, in the same questionnaire, is provided in Table 7.2. The example is a questionnaire that asks students undertaking a research methods course to indicate what they intend to do for their assignment. The assignment is a detailed proposal for their dissertation, which they will start at a later date. The questionnaire also asks students to think through how confident they are about the decisions they have made about their proposal. (You might want to use this questionnaire to help you think about your own research.)

Table 7.2 Example of an integrated approach to asking closed and open questions

Preparing for your assignment ...	... how confident are you?			
Please answer the questions by writing in your answer. Then circle one number only that represents how confident you feel about your answer.	Extremely	Fairly	Unsure	Not at all confident
1 What is the substantive focus (i.e. subject/topic) of your research? ✍	1	2	3	4
2 What is your research question? ✍	1	2	3	4
3 Where will your research take place? ✍	1	2	3	4
4 On what concepts or theories will you draw? ✍	1	2	3	4
5 Who or what are your sources of data? ✍	1	2	3	4
6 What method(s) of data collection will you use? ✍	1	2	3	4
7 What type(s) of data will you collect? ✍	1	2	3	4

To help you think through how you might manage the integration of different approaches to asking questions, the following is a brief for a research project.

The brief

The Certificate in Inter-professional Research Methodology is a part-time, one year post-graduate professional course. There are 60 students currently enrolled on the course and the next start date is in around six months from now.

Traditionally, the course has been taught using face-to-face lectures, with supporting tutorials. The course consists of three modules, each twenty credits in length. Module three is entitled Innovations in Data Collection and lasts over 10 weekly meetings during term three. Each meeting is timetabled for two hours. The assessment is through an end-of-module assignment of 5,000 words.

As part of the ongoing development of the programme, the course team has decided to introduce an online version of the Innovations in Data Collection module. As part of the development activities, it has been agreed to undertake an evaluation of the student experience on the new module. Some members of the course team, for example, believe that students will not be very happy about the change and this will result in a high drop-out rate in subsequent years.

Your task

You are asked, therefore, to evaluate the student experience on the new online module, Innovations in Data Collection, during its first presentation which starts in a few months' time.

Part of your task will be to explain what methods of data collection you would use to ensure the evaluation of the student experience provides a detailed insight into the views of the students. So, you have decided that you will undertake the evaluative data collection in three stages.

A possible response to the brief

In Stage 1, the method of data collection will be a web-based electronic questionnaire that all course participants are invited to complete. Each would receive an email with the URL (unique resource locator) at which the questionnaire can be located. Figure 7.1 shows the first page of the questionnaire. This is part of a survey in www.surveymonkey.com and would be quite easy to compile given the design templates available on the site.

The purpose of the questionnaire in Stage 1 is to provide an insight into the initial views of the participants as the module gets underway. It also provides information about their previous use of online questionnaires.

In Stage 2, a paper-based questionnaire would provide the participants with an opportunity to start to evaluate their own experiences of the module. The questionnaire would contain only four open questions:

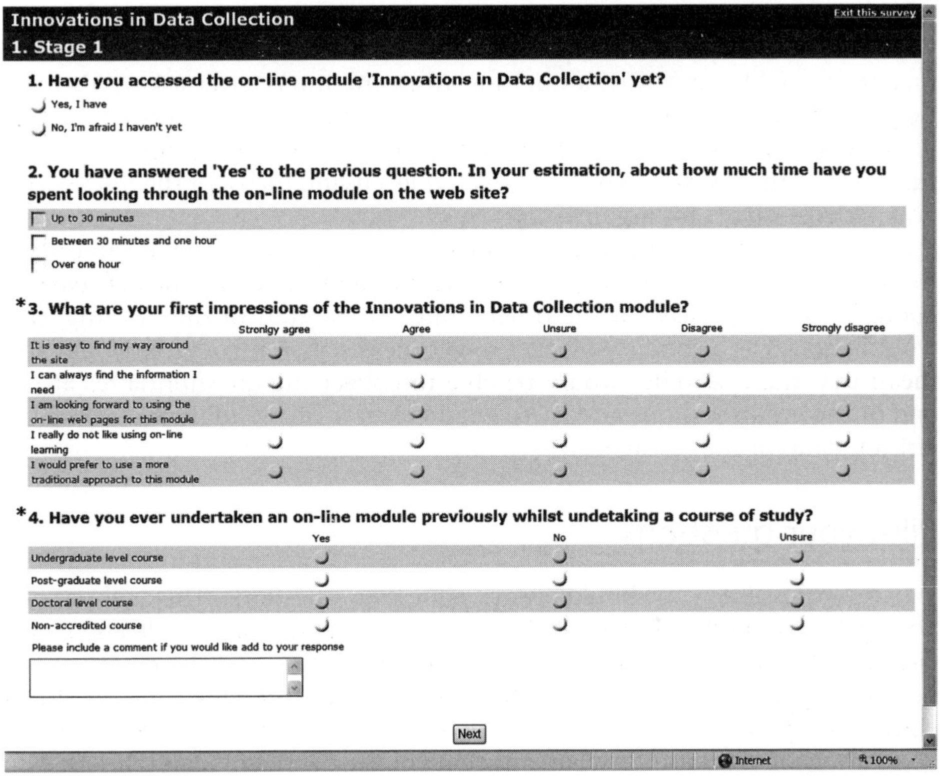

Figure 7.1 Stage 1 electronic questionnaire

1 As you approach the end of the module, please write a few notes about what you feel have been the positive experiences of undertaking the online module, *Innovations in Data Collection*.
2 As you approach the end of the module, please write a few notes about what you feel have been the negative experiences of undertaking the online module, *Innovations in Data Collection*.
3 For future presentations of the module, what aspects of the module would you want to see changed and why?
4 Which elements would you like to see kept in the module and why?

The questions are presented on two sides of A4-sized paper, with space for the respondents' replies.

The questionnaire would be sent in the post or perhaps handed out to students during class. It might be distributed via email, since there would be an up-to-date sampling frame of email addresses which could be used. Participants would be asked to complete the questionnaire as fully as possible by writing in their replies. They would also be asked to bring the completed questionnaire along with them when they attended the group discussions two weeks after the course finishes.

In Stage 3 of the research, a number of group discussions would take place, based on the analysis of the questionnaires from Stages 1 and 2. The group meetings would begin with a question from the interviewer asking the participants to talk through their replies to the Stage 2 questionnaires. The researcher would also be able to share with the groups the findings from the first stage of the research. This would provide a useful focus for the discussions and perhaps points for argument.

Sending the questionnaire out before the meeting would provide an opportunity for a relatively high degree of thought and reflection by the participants about their experiences on the programme. At the start of the meeting, this would also act as a good ice-breaker to get the discussion going. It would also mean that the researcher would be able to collect the questionnaires at the end of the group sessions and these would then form an additional source of written data for the research.

Pilot your questions

Wherever possible, you should always pilot your questions. This will provide you with an opportunity to test that the decisions you have made about this element of your research are correct. The pilot can focus on the clarity of the questions, the design and style of the way you have presented the questions electronically or on paper, and anything else that you might be unsure about. You may want to pilot those elements that you *are* confident about, just in case you are wrong! However, you may not have the time nor the resources to pilot everything about your questions! It will be a matter of being selective about what you can manage in the available time and within your financial budget.

How do you go about organising a pilot? Well, Simmons argues that:

> As a guide, in a proposed survey of 2,000 respondents, the pilot sample should include between 10 and 20 respondents. This initial group must have similar characteristics to those of the population to be studied. From the pilot, the researcher will be able to assess whether the line of questioning is appropriate and whether the document is understandable and simple to use. (2001: 103)

The important thing to remember about a pilot study is that it should inform your approach to the main research. This means that, in your final report, you should spend some time explaining what you piloted, what the outcomes were and how these impacted on your subsequent methodology. You should keep this as brief as possible.

Using pilot study data

One question that most researchers need to answer about their *pilot* study is whether or not the findings should be used in the *main* study. As you would expect, there is no definitive answer to this question! If the participants in your pilot have been drawn from the same research population as the sample that you intend to use for the main research, then it is legitimate to include the data in the main analysis. However, there may be problems associated with this. For example, as a result of the pilot study, you may change your questions or the methods of data collection. In addition, you might revisit and subsequently amend your main research question. In these cases, you would not include the data from your pilot study. This is because you are, in effect, carrying out a different piece of research, so it would probably not be legitimate to include the pilot data.

If, however, the pilot study confirms your decisions about the approach and the methods, then it will be safe to include the pilot data. It would also be acceptable to include the pilot data if you have, say, interviewed or sent a questionnaire to a large enough sample. Here, you would be on safe ground if you counted the pilot study as a separate stage in the research and analysed and reported on the data separately. You would still be expected to declare that it was a pilot study and not the main part of your research.

The conclusion, therefore, is that if you are confident that the pilot study is the same research as the main study, then you will be justified in using the pilot data. If you are not confident, then you should not incorporate the data into your research, except to explain how it informed the decisions you made about your main study.

Summary 7.3

- When using the FraIM, build in closed and open questions that collect both narrative and numerical data.
- Closed questions are based on the researcher's agenda.
- Open questions give respondents an opportunity to decide for themselves what to write about.
- Wherever possible pilot your questions.
- A pilot study aims to inform the approach to the main research.
- Your research report should include an explanation of the pilot, in particular what you did, what the outcomes were and what impact the outcomes had on your subsequent methodology.
- There will be occasions when you may be able to use the data from your pilot study in the main study.

Conclusion

This chapter has discussed the use of asking questions as a method of data collection. The questions can either be written or spoken and delivered in a number of different ways, including face-to-face, paper-based and electronically. The chapter also argued that it is possible to integrate the different approaches to asking questions by employing a participant-centred strategy. In addition, both closed and open questions can be used. The former are based on the researcher's agenda and the latter give respondents an opportunity to decide for themselves what information to provide. Finally, it was argued that wherever possible questions should be piloted.

The next chapter now moves on to considering the third method of data collection: artefact analysis.

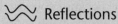 Reflections

1 To what extent will you integrate the different approaches to asking questions in your research, using written and spoken questions employing face-to-face, paper and electronic media?

Asking questions	My research
Written	
Face-to-face: paper	
Face-to-face: electronic	
Face-to-face: paper:	
electronic	
Paper: electronic	
Spoken	
Face-to-face: paper	
Face-to-face: electronic	
Face-to-face: paper: electronic	
Paper: electronic	

Associated reading

- Bell, J. (2002) 'Questionnaires', Chapter 10 in M. Coleman and A.R.J. Briggs (eds), *Research Methods in Educational Leadership*. London: SAGE.
- Bryman, A. (2008) *Social Research Methods* (3rd edn). Oxford: Oxford University Press. See Chapter 10, 'Asking questions'.
- Finch, H. and Lewis, J. (2003) 'Focus groups', Chapter 7 in J. Ritchie and J. Lewis (eds), *Qualitative Research Practice: A Guide for Social Science Students and Researchers*. London: SAGE.
- Gillham, B. (2005) *Research Interviewing: The Range of Techniques*. Maidenhead: Open University Press.
- Legard, R., Keegan, J. and Ward, K. (2003) 'In-depth interviews', Chapter 6 in J. Ritchie and J. Lewis (eds), *Qualitative Research Practice: A Guide for Social Science Students and Researchers*. London: SAGE.
- Mann, C. and Stewart, F. (2003) 'Internet interviewing', Chapter 5 in J.F. Gubrium and J.A. Holstein (eds), *Postmodern Interviewing*. London: SAGE.
- Oppenheim, A. (2000) *Questionnaire Design, Interviewing and Attitude Measurement*. London: Continuum.
- Wragg, T. (2002) 'Interviewing', Chapter 9 in M. Coleman and A.R.J. Briggs (eds), *Research Methods in Educational Leadership*. London: SAGE.

Analysing artefacts I

This chapter will:

- present a number of selected issues associated with analysing documents, images and other artefacts
- explain what an artefact is in the context of the FraIM
- outline the processes involved in analysing artefacts as the basis of undertaking educational and social research
- provide examples that will enable you to use artefact analysis in your own research.

Introduction

By now, you probably won't need reminding that an integrated research methodology argues that there are three types of methods of data generation and collection: observation, asking questions and artefact analysis. This chapter looks specifically at the third method: artefact analysis. This is an area of research that tends not to find its way into the majority of methodology textbooks. It sometimes gets a mention, but rarely in any detail. Because of that, you may not have had an opportunity to read much about it. Therefore, this book dedicates two whole chapters to the subject.

The first point to make is that the different characteristics associated with observation and asking questions, outlined in Chapter 5, apply equally to artefact analysis. These are degree of structure and level of mediation. Remember that the former determines the level of pre-structuring of the data collected and the latter the metaphorical distance of the researcher to the phenomena being studied. Table 8.1 provides a comparison of the different methods based on the unfolding of the research process.

From Table 8.1, you may feel that a more suitable name for this approach might be artefact *deconstruction* rather than analysis, reflecting a more accurate description of the processes involved in this third method of data collection. However, terms such as documentary *analysis* and textual *analysis* are used extensively in the literature to label what is here called 'artefact analysis'.

Table 8.1   Comparison of methods of data collection

Method of data collection	Data sources	Main process focus	Examples of outcomes
		Unfolding of the research process ──────▶	
Observation	Participants	Observation	–Field notes –Counts of behaviour –Description of activities
Asking questions	Informants	Interrogation	–Questionnaire results –Interview transcripts
Artefact analysis	Artefacts	Deconstruction	–Descriptive and analytical accounts of items –Counts of characteristics of items –Measures of amounts of characteristics of items

This term, therefore, will be used, while at the same time acknowledging its inadequacy in capturing the true nature of the processes involved.

Whatever label we choose to use, the main activity or process involved in artefact analysis is that of deconstruction which generates the raw data that are collected, analysed and interpreted.

Deconstruction involves critically examining the relationships between the elements of an artefact with the artefact as a whole. This is described in some detail below.

What is an artefact?

So, what then is an artefact and what are the characteristics of artefacts? First of all, artefacts are those objects or events that are produced by people. Table 8.2 lists a number of examples of artefacts. As you can see, the categorisation is based partly on sensory experience. It also includes examples of text-based artefacts and those drawing on what can be referred to as a kinaesthetic or spatial dimension.

Table 8.2   Examples of artefacts

Text	Visual	Sound	Kinaesthetic/spatial	Smell	Taste
Books	Photographs	Radio	Theatre	Food	Food
Newspapers	Drawings	Music	Dance	Drink	Drink
Magazines	Illustrations	Videos			
Web page	Films	Films			
Texts (SMS)	Videos				
Letters	Clothes				
Prospectuses	Buildings				
Leaflets	Interiors				
Brochures	Décor				

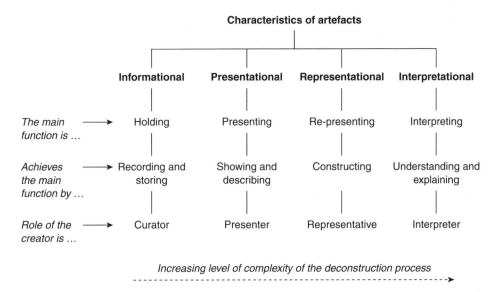

Figure 8.1 Types of artefacts

The examples listed range from static written texts to visual and sound imagery, through to real-life dynamic events or performances that occupy space and, at times, can involve movement. One immediate impression from Table 8.2 is that artefacts can include information from different media. In other words, the categories are not necessarily mutually exclusive. For example, a video film can include visual imagery, music, speech, sound effects and text in the form of credits or captions.

So, the collection of different artefacts and their possible combinations provide quite a challenge to any self-respecting mainstream researcher out to make a name for themselves. However, as a researcher using the FraIM, you would expect such a complex and sophisticated combination of different factors.

Characteristics of artefacts

Artefacts have four main characteristics that are relevant to their use in research. These are:

- informational
- presentational
- representational
- interpretational.

The four different characteristics are defined by their main function. These are outlined in Figure 8.1.

It can be argued that there is a hierarchy of complexity associated with artefact characteristics. The most straightforward is informational and the most complex is interpretational. The same artefact can potentially function at different levels. However, a higher level will entail each of the lower levels.

Informational artefact

An informational artefact is the least complex of artefacts and occupies the lowest level of conceptual and methodological sophistication of use in research. Its main function is to hold information until it is needed. It achieves this through the recording and storing of information. An example would be the diary entries that you might keep as part of your research. Another example might be a message kept on a personal digital recorder. The role of the creator of an informational artefact is that of a curator or keeper of information.

Presentational artefact

The main function of a presentational artefact is to present information to others. This is achieved through showing and describing ideas, events, information, knowledge and understanding. The purpose of the creation of this type of artefact is to share the information with others. It goes beyond the mere recording and storage of that information.

An example would be a letter or email that you might use to communicate with someone. Other examples might be the informational or instructional notices found on an organisation's notice boards. These might be in a hospitable or a school. Further examples, could be a radio or TV news programme or a newspaper article. A presentational artefact functions at a *denotative* level of meaning since there is no attempt to go beyond the 'surface meaning' of the signs and elements in the artefact.

The role of the creator of a presentational artefact is that of a presenter. Put simply, this is someone who shows information or simply presents or describes it to someone else.

Representational artefact

The main function of a representational artefact is to *re-present* information to others through the presentation or re-presentation of selected ideas, events, information, knowledge and understanding. The purpose of the creation of this type of artefact is to offer a construction of our understanding of particular social contexts or events or experiences.

Representational artefacts are often considered to be *cultural* artefacts. They 'stand in' for other things. Examples would be a series of photographs in a family album, a TV commercial or a children's storybook. A photograph will depict or re-present a scene or person. A TV commercial may re-present a particular way of life or series of relationships between the characters depicted on the screen. A children's storybook might re-present the idea of friendship between humans and animals. They draw on particular discourses for their identity and characteristics and will go beyond the surface meaning of the signs they employ by using connotational meaning to achieve their effects and impact.

You should note also that the same artefact can have both presentational and representational characteristics. For example, a radio or TV news programme or a newspaper article can have both presentational and representational functions. A photograph, too, can present information, for example, as a record of a family gathering or a well-deserved graduation ceremony.

Representational artefacts build on the techniques of the recording, storage and presentation of information that are characteristics of lower order artefacts.

The role of the creator of a representational artefact is that of a representative. This is someone who acts or speaks on behalf of others. They achieve this through the process of authorship of the artefact. Creating an artefact, they are responsible for re-presenting the information or their experiences or their understanding to a readership or audience.

Interpretational artefact

An artefact with an interpretational function occupies the highest order on the dimension of artefacts. The process of creation and generation of the artefact goes further than drawing on an informational, presentational and representational perspective.

As the term suggests, its main function is to offer an *interpretation* of the issues under study. Its purpose is the creation of artefacts that, as with the previous category, are often referred to and discussed as *cultural* artefacts. Such artefacts re-present and interpret the social and cultural worlds we are part of. They present and continually re-present those interpretations to us through drawing on the commonly and intuitively understood symbols, signs and discourses of the societies in which we live.

The role of the creator of an interpretational artefact is that of an 'interpreter'. The most important aspect of an interpreter's role is to implicitly or explicitly explain the *meaning* of, for example, an event or experience, by offering an interpretation or translation of that experience. This process is based on understanding and explaining the meaning of the experience or event through the creation of artefacts.

Example of the four levels

When you plan your research, it will be important to start with a clear idea of the focus of your interest. It may be the representation of gender in magazine

Figure 8.2   Living accommodation in poor, rural South Africa

advertisements or how children's stories portray the family in western culture. You may be interested in developing an insight into the perspectives of the informants in your research using, say, participants' diaries or paintings. Figure 8.2 is a photograph of living accommodation in a poor, rural area of an African country.

An analysis of the photograph indicates the following:

- *Informational function*: the photograph is a record of a visit to a poor, rural area of an African country
- *Presentational function*: the photograph may be shown to other family members or is part of, for example, a meeting of amateur photographers or shown during a geography degree course teaching session
- *Representational function*: the photograph portrays and depicts the environment and a particular way of living in an African location
- *Interpretational function*: the photograph uses a variety of signs and symbols and draws on particular visual discourses, enabling us to derive meaning from the photograph.

Summary 8.1

- Artefacts range from static written texts and visual and sound imagery to real-life dynamic events and performances.
- Artefacts have four main characteristics, defined by their function:

  - informational
  - presentational
  - representational
  - interpretational.

- There is an increasing level of complexity from informational to interpretational artefacts.
- The main process used in artefact analysis is that of deconstruction.
- Deconstruction involves analysis of an artefact's constituent elements.

What is artefact analysis?

The rest of this chapter and the next, Chapter 9, describes in more detail the processes involved in three different approaches to artefact analysis. The chapter begins with an overview of what these approaches are and then looks at the integrating processes that underlie artefact analysis.

Using the FraIM, it is possible to bring these different approaches together. It allows, indeed encourages, you to take a more integrated approach when undertaking research aimed at deconstructing informational, presentational, representational and interpretational artefacts.

First of all, however, both this chapter and the next look briefly at what each of these methods involves. Because of the complexity of the approaches, these chapters can only give you a flavour of the main ideas associated with each one. In addition, you should bear in mind that there are other approaches to analysing artefacts apart from the three reported here.

Less structured approaches: semiotic analysis

Inevitably, due to the complex ideas associated with semiotics, the account that follows is a somewhat simplified one.

There are two approaches to semiotics. The first was developed by the American Charles Sanders Peirce (1839–1914) and has its origins in philosophy. It was aimed at developing an understanding and explanation of how we come to understand the world through the study of signs (Nöth, 1995).

The second, which developed independently although round about the same time, is 'semiology'. This is associated with Ferdinand de Saussure (1857–1913) who lived in Geneva in Switzerland. It is based on the study of linguistics and was originally aimed at developing a general theory of language (Gottdiener, 1995). For a variety of reasons, Peirce's semiotics is the more appropriate for the purposes of this chapter. However, if you want to read further about Saussure's semiology, then please refer to the suggestions at the end of the chapter.

Peirce's semiotics

Semiotics is interested in the meaning of signs and the process of signification, or semeiosis, where a sign can be anything that stands for something else (Cobley and Jansz, 2004). 'Signs take the form of words, images, sounds, gestures and objects' (Chandler, 2002: 2). They can also be aromas and tastes, although these are not commonly considered alongside the use of the other senses. A brief example of a smell standing for something else is perfume, which can have the aroma of roses or musk or a variety of other objects. If you're a vegetarian, then you'll be familiar with the taste of food that is meant to simulate or represent the taste of meat.

Signs include words. The marks on this page (or screen, if you're looking at an electronic version) are signs, since they form the words that stand for ideas and objects. In turn, the word 'dog', for example, denotes or means a four-legged animal. A photograph of a national flag denotes the flag itself, but also has connotational associations of patriotism or, under some circumstances, hatred and xenophobia.

Peirce's theory is a very detailed system that attempts to make sense of our experiences of the world. He was a philosopher interested in epistemology, the theory of knowledge, and he is credited with being one of the founding members of the pragmatist movement. This is covered in more detail in Chapter 14.

Peirce's semiotics is a triadic model consisting of sign, interpretant and object. It will be worth quoting Peirce directly to provide an explanation of what this means:

> A sign or representamen is something which stands to somebody for something in some respect or capacity. It addresses somebody, that is, creates in the mind of that person an equivalent sign, or perhaps a more developed sign. That which it creates I call the interpretant of the first sign. The sign stands for something, its object. It stands for that object, not in all respects, but in reference to a sort of idea. (1932: 228)

Perhaps his explanation isn't too clear, so Figure 8.3 provides a summary of this process, which Peirce referred to as *semeiosis*. It is based on three elements: a sign, an object and an interpretant. Semeiosis is the process whereby signs acquire meaning for someone by becoming associated with an object.

The sign represents or stands for an object. It can only do this as a result of there being someone – an interpreter – who sees, hears, tastes, smells or comes into physical contact with the sign. As a result of the interpretation process, the interpreter develops an understanding of what the sign stands for. In other words, the sign acquires meaning for the person, the interpreter.

As you can see from Figure 8.3, objects occupy two categories or classifications; the immediate and the mediate. The *mediate* object is the actual, real, existing object to which the sign refers. For example, the word 'cat' refers to a four-legged animal with, for example, black hair and very sharp claws and teeth. However, to know that there is a connection between the two, you

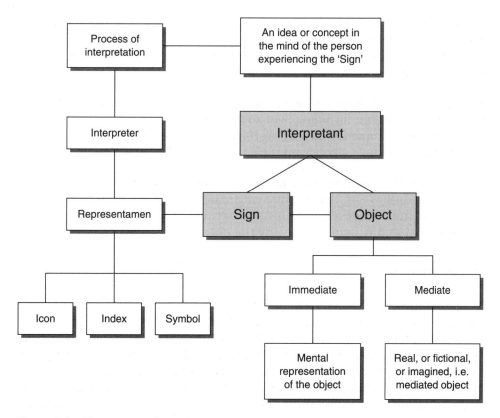

Figure 8.3 The process of semeiosis

would picture, think about or conceptualise this real animal, the cat. This concept, or mental representation of the object, is the *immediate* object.

There are three types of representamen or signs: the icon, the index and the symbol.

An *icon* resembles or attempts to imitate the object by looking, sounding, tasting, smelling or feeling like it. An obvious example is a photograph. A young child holding out his arms horizontally and imitating the sound of droning engines while running around the school playground pretending to be an aeroplane is an example of visual and auditory iconic signs. The small icons on your computer desktop that look like, say, a folder are iconic signs that represent electronic storage space on your hard drive. The same principle applies to the picture of an envelope on your email system that looks like a paper envelope.

A *symbol* has an arbitrary relationship with the object it represents. It does not look, sound, taste, smell or feel like the object. The link between a symbol and the object has to be learned. The most obvious example is language where, for example, the word 'cat' bears no resemblance to a real cat. Another example would be the picture of a heart that symbolises the emotional state of love, or a skull and crossbones that symbolises the fear and terror of the state of lawlessness. Organisations spend a lot of money on developing a corporate identity which includes the use of a logo. You will be able to picture in your mind's eye a number of established logos that symbolise companies or organisations that are known throughout the world, for example, Coca Cola, McDonalds or Nike. Perhaps you can think of others?

An *index* or indexical sign has a causative link with the object. Chandler (2002: 37) lists:

- natural signs, such as smoke, thunder, footprints, non-synthetic odours and flavours
- medical symptoms, including pain and pulse rates
- measuring instruments, such as weathercocks, thermometers, clocks
- signals, for example a knock on the door or a telephone ringing.

Smoke is an index of fire, pulse rate is an index of physical exertion, a thermometer indicates the temperature of a room and a knock is an index of someone being outside a room on the other side of the door. In other words, the indexical sign is *caused directly* by the object.

Visual images

One common use of Peirce's semiotics is its application to the analysis of visual images. An example of this is provided by Figure 8.2. As you have already seen, the photograph is of living accommodation in rural South Africa. The small truck in the background is a relatively cheap bukky pick-up truck, a common sight on the roads in South Africa. Although you cannot see from this black and white reproduction, the colours are light-coloured sand and a faded green and dulled yellow from the shrubs and tree flowers. The photograph portrays isolation, barrenness and poverty. These cannot be explicitly seen in the image itself, of course, but can be *inferred* from the visual elements of the photograph, especially if you have knowledge of the context, which in this example is poor rural South Africa. Indeed, inferring meaning from an image's observable, constituent elements, that is, the signs, is at the heart of all approaches to artefact analysis. This is sometimes described as making inferences from the *manifest* content to the underlying *latent* content of ideas, values and concepts. The manifest content is the observable elements or signs of the artefact. The latent content is the underlying meaning that the artefact can reveal on closer examination and through the process of deconstruction mentioned earlier.

▢ Summary 8.2

- The main less structured methods of artefact analysis are semiotic analysis and discourse analysis.
- The main structured approach is referred to as content analysis.
- Historically, there are two main theories associated with semiotic analysis: semiology, from the linguist Ferdinand de Saussure, and semiotics, associated with the pragmatist philosopher, Charles Sanders Peirce.
- Peirce's system of semiotics is used with the FraIM and is based on a sign, an interpretant and an object.

Less structured approaches: discourse analysis

A second approach to artefact analysis using a less structured method is that of discourse analysis. MacLure (2003) argues that there are two strands to discourse analysis based on different histories and agendas. These are, first, discourse analysis which is taken from the study of linguistics and is firmly embedded in a structuralist perspective, and, second, an alternative, post-structuralist approach.

The former is characterised by an analytic process that focuses on the words, sentences and internal structure of textual artefacts with the purpose of explaining the meaning of written and spoken texts. It involves 'the study of language, in the everyday sense in which most people use the term [language]' (Johnstone, 2002: 2). Cameron defines it as 'language above the sentence … [which] means it looks for patterns (structure, organisation) in units which are larger, more extended, than one sentence' (2001: 11).

The second approach to discourse analysis, mentioned by MacLure, is characterised by 'a radical suspicion of reason, order and certainty as governing principles of knowledge and existence' (2003: 180) and it can lead to the exposure of hegemonic ideology expressed through the use of language. This type of discourse analysis is usually referred to as *critical* discourse analysis, which is about 'analysing opaque as well as transparent structural relationships of dominance, discrimination, power and control as manifested in language … [and] … aims to investigate critically social inequality as it is expressed, signalled, constituted, legitimized and so on by language use' (Wodak and Meyer, 2001: 2).

Critical discourse analysis is more relevant to the research you would undertake based on the FraIM. It requires you to 'suspend your disbelief in the innocence of words and the transparency of language as a window on an objectively graspable reality' (MacLure, 2003: 12). This implies that words and language do more than express ideas that mirror what we talk or write about. They are inextricably linked with the way we interact with and develop an understanding of the world. Further, that interaction is based on an understanding that is structured by language as well as other types of experiences. The context and the range of experiences on which we draw, in order to understand the meanings we create through language, are the basis of the linguistic discourses we use and in which we are immersed. Johnstone even goes as far as arguing that 'Anyone who wants to understand human beings has to understand discourse' (2002: 7).

Coyle's definition may be particularly useful in helping to understand what linguistic discourses are. He states that:

> discourses can be defined as sets of linguistic material that have a degree of coherence in their content and organization and which perform constructive functions in broadly defined social contexts. (2007: 101)

Wetherell offers a more simple explanation, arguing that 'discourse is talk, language in use and human meaning-making activities' (2001: 27).

The important characteristic that these authors draw attention to is that discourse functions to construct social meaning from our experiences and activities.

Summary 8.3

- Discourse analysis is a less structured approach to artefact analysis. It draws on two main approaches.
- One is based on the study of linguistics and aims to explain the meaning of written and spoken texts through the study of everyday language used in particular contexts.
- A second approach is critical discourse analysis, which aims to expose the inequalities between social groups manifested through language use.
- Discourse analysis is based on the view that discourse constructs social meaning from our experiences and activities.

Foucault may be helpful, too, in enabling us to understand the nature and meaning of discourse. His perspective, however, goes beyond the analysis of discourse as text and language. He was interested in how discourse generates knowledge and meaning at a macro, that is, societal level (Hall, 2001), and, further, how it exerts an invisible power and an often insidious – and invidious – control over human relationships at all levels of society.

Foucault's concern with discourse, knowledge and power is highly relevant to undertaking research based on the analysis of artefacts. Hall (2001) points out that when we are confronted with knowledge that is linked to and supported by power, we assume that such knowledge is true. Power, in this case, comes from the social and political institutions that are part and parcel of our culture and ways of living. We accept them as legitimate and, through that legitimacy, they acquire and exert power over our lives.

Usually, most people find it difficult to challenge many of the ideas about how we live and conduct our lives. The dominant culture we are part of and which we help to perpetuate appears quite natural to us. Artefacts, including linguistic texts, are part of that culture. The role of the researcher using artefact analysis is to critically analyse those artefacts and come to an understanding of what they tell us about the cultures within which we live and operate as individuals and as a society over time.

It is the role of the artefact analyst to see through the surface meanings of the artefacts. Their task is to critically challenge the ideas and ideologies that are presented and re-presented by those artefacts and raise searching questions about the interpretations of the culture and ways of living that the artefacts are offering to us.

Figure 8.4 provides a summary framework that is based on these ideas. It outlines the process whereby discourse functions to inform, present, re-present

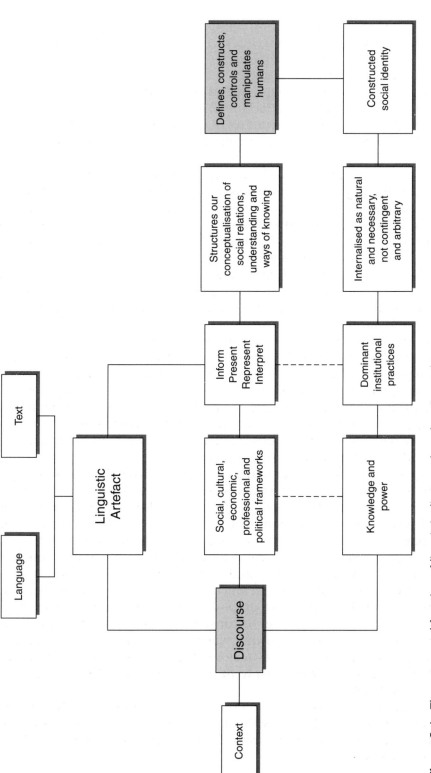

Figure 8.4 The nature and function of linguistic discourse based on Foucault

and interpret knowledge and meaning about our experience of the world. The framework focuses on linguistic artefacts where discourse draws on language and text. In this framework, language consists of linguistic elements, that is, words, phrases and sentences of written and spoken artefacts that are systematically combined together by rules and conventions, to produce 'extended stretches of talk or writing' (MacLure, 2003: 182). The manifestation of the text or the physical object, recording or presentation of the text, is the artefact. The artefact is located in particular discourses, which are always located in and embedded in specific contexts.

Any discourse will draw on the kaleidoscope of social, cultural, economic, professional and political frameworks that inform the identity and experience of the society in which we live. Thus, the processes of informing about, presenting, re-presenting and interpreting ideological and dominant institutional practices, through the use of artefacts, structure our conceptualisation of social relations, understanding and ways of knowing. This enables discourses to define, construct, control, manipulate and position us in both the social world and the natural world. Wetherell argues that it does this through building or *constructing* objects, worlds, minds and social relations rather than simply *reflecting* them (2001:16).

The interesting thing about this process, however, is that our constructed social identities eventually become internalised as natural and necessary, not contingent and arbitrary. In other words, our identities, our social relations, our ways of thinking and our attitudes, values and beliefs are experienced as being the only natural way to live. There are no alternatives. It is natural that we experience social identity in the way we do and live the way we live, taking part in a range of social relations that have their own built-in 'natural' rules about what is allowable and what is not.

They appear to us to be so much a part of our lives that we do not even think that there may be alternatives. That is because the practices of our main societal institutions such as the law, political system, family and social relationships, education, sexuality and many others have an insidious power and control over our thinking and behaviour. At times, this control and power is not even explicit or overt. We 'police' ourselves because we know how to think and behave in a particular context and at a particular time in our history, in much the same way that Jeremy Bentham's Panopticon worked. This was a proposed nineteenth century prison design that allows an unseen observer to constantly observe and monitor prisoners without the prisoners knowing when exactly they are being watched. Inmates of the prison know they may be observed at any time, and with that in mind, modify their behaviour to fit the institution's rules and regulations (Bentham, 1843).

It is how the ruling government exercises an insidious and invidious power and control over our lives – without us knowing that it is exercising that control and power. One of the ways it achieves this is through the role that discourses play in our lives.

Non-linguistic discourses

The above section explored the role of language in discourse analysis. Language, however, is the basis of only one of a number of different types of discourse. Cartoon strips, advertising, television, film, gardens and even the human body can all be considered to constitute discourse practices that can be a fruitful source of data analysis for research purposes (Parker, 1999: 3). Each discourse is informed by and informs the process of signification that was outlined in the earlier section on semiotics.

Conclusion

The role of the artefact analyst is to develop a deeper and critical understanding of the ideological values expressed by social and cultural artefacts. This chapter introduced you to two important methods of achieving this understanding: semiotics and discourse analysis. When you use these strategies you will be taking a relatively less structured approach to data collection and analysis in your research. In contrast, the next chapter examines, in some detail, a *structured* approach to analysing artefacts.

 Reflections

1 Select two or three print advertisements or alternatively, choose two or three of your favourite photographs and/or illustrations.
2 Describe each one under the functional headings of informational, presentational, representational and interpretational artefacts.
3 How useful a distinction do you find these four categories of artefact? Please explain your answer.
4 If you are considering using artefact analysis in your own research, explain the procedures you will use.

Associated reading

- Belsey, C. (2005) 'Textual analysis as a research method', Chapter 9 in G. Griffin (ed.), *Research Methods for English Studies*. Edinburgh: Edinburgh University Press.
- Chandler, D. (2002) *Semiotics: The Basics*. Routledge: London.
- Cobley, P. and Jansz, L. (2004) *Introducing Semiotics*. Royston: Icon Books.
- Fairclough, N. (1995) *Critical Discourse Analysis: The Critical Study of Language*. London: Longman.
- MacLure, M. (2003) *Discourse in Educational and Social Research*. Maidenhead: Open University Press.

- Pink, S. (2007) *Doing Visual Ethnography: Images, Media and Representation in Research* (2nd edn). London: SAGE.
- Potter, J. (2004) 'Discourse analysis as a way of analysing naturally occurring talk', Chapter 11 in D. Silverman (ed.), *Qualitative Research: Theory, Method and Practice*. London: SAGE.
- Rose, G. (2007) *Visual Methodologies: An Introduction to the Interpretation of Visual Materials* (2nd edn). London: SAGE.
- deSaussure, F. (1972) *Course in General Linguistics*. Edited by C. Bally and A. Sechehaye with the collaboration of A. Riedlinger. Translated by R. Harris. London: Duckworth.
- Wetherell, M., Taylor, S. and Yates, S.J. (eds) (2001) *Discourse Theory and Practice: A Reader*. London: SAGE.
- Wodak, R. and Meyer, M. (2001) *Methods of Critical Discourse Analysis*. London: SAGE.

Analysing artefacts II

This chapter will:

- describe a structured approach to artefact analysis which is usually referred to as content analysis
- present an integrated approach to combining content analysis, discourse analysis and semiotic analysis
- argue for the importance of abductive inference in artefact analysis
- provide examples to enable you to use artefact analysis in your own research.

Introduction

In the previous chapter you read about the characteristics of artefacts and a brief explanation of what artefact analysis entails. This was followed by an explanation of two relatively less structured approaches to this method of data collection. These were semiotic analysis and discourse analysis. This chapter now outlines a procedure for a third approach: content analysis. It then presents a way of integrating all three approaches to artefact analysis.

A structured approach to artefact analysis

Content analysis falls under the heading of a structured approach to data collection. This involves applying a closed coding schedule that results in a count or a measure of the elements of interest in the artefact being analysed. For example, Hodson points out that 'the researcher might code the prevalence in the documents of certain words or certain ideas. Words, themes and ideas can then be correlated across documents and patterns established' (1999: 6).

Content analysis is frequently used in the analysis of media output and might include, for example, counting the number of acts of aggression or violence in a TV programme or children's comic story. Arguments are then put forward about the effects of watching such acts on the behaviour of viewers. Holsti has defined this type of content analysis as 'any technique for making inferences by objectively and systematically identifying specified characteristics of messages' (1969: 14).

An interesting, early definition of content analysis comes from Berelson, who stated that: 'Content analysis is a research technique for the objective, systematic and quantitative description of the manifest content of communication' (1952: 18). A more recent perspective is provided by Neuendorf who defines content analysis as a 'summarizing, quantitative analysis of messages that relies on the scientific method ... and is not limited as to the types of variables that may be measured or the context in which the messages are created or presented' (2002: 10).

Both of these definitions make it clear that content analysis is to be used with messages or communication materials. This is unnecessarily restrictive. There is no logical reason why content analysis should not be considered to be applicable to all types of artefacts and not just those whose main function is to intentionally convey messages. For example, content analysis can be used to categorise pupils' diary entries that they may have written each week as part of a literacy project. This was, in fact, mentioned earlier in Chapter 2.

Another focus of Berelson's definition is that content analysis is a study of the *manifest* content of messages. This is an idea you came across in the previous Chapter. Researchers in this area have moved on since the 1950s, with authors (such as Krippendorff, 2004) disagreeing with this exclusive focus on only what can be seen or heard.

Manifest content is usually contrasted with *latent* content, that is, the hidden or deeper meanings underlying the observable elements in an artefact. The task of undertaking a content analysis, therefore, might be to identify the manifest content in order to infer what the latent content might be. Again, this was mentioned in the previous chapter.

If you use content analysis in your research, it is likely that you will be interested in developing an understanding of the patterns of elements within and across a sample of the same type of artefact. Some work I carried out a while ago, in the 1980s, investigated the way that technology was presented in television advertisements (Plowright, 1991). A sample of TV commercials was taken between December 1984 and January 1985. On alternate evenings between 6 pm and 11 pm every advertisement broadcast by a regional television company in the UK was recorded. This gave a total of 28 days of advertisements. On average, approximately 80 advertisements per evening were broadcast during this time, giving a total of 2,240. For the analysis, any that were repeated were ignored. In the end, a final sample of 270 was used for the study.

A closed coding schedule was employed for the analysis. This allowed the identification of salient elements of each and every one of the 270 commercials. First of all, the advertisements were categorised as promoting either technology or non-technology products. These were then identified as communications products or general products. Figure 9.1 shows further details of how the products were categorised and examples of each category.

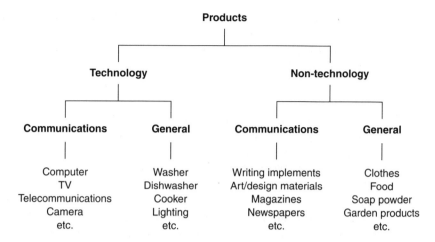

Figure 9.1   Product categorisation with examples

Additional analyses included identifying the gender and ages of the figures appearing in the commercials. Subsequently, cross-tabulations carried out on the data revealed that the highest proportion of any category of figure appearing in television commercials for all communications technology products was that of young adult males. Other age groups did not play a major part in this technological world. It was a time when the use of communications and information technologies was not as widespread as they are today. But from these findings we can infer that at that time, the developing image of communications technologies portrayed was a young man's world, with very little involvement of females or other age ranges.

Summary 9.1

- Content analysis is a structured approach to data collection.
- It uses a closed coding schedule resulting in a count or a measure of the elements of interest in an artefact.
- It can be used with all types of artefacts.
- It studies the manifest content of artefacts, which is contrasted with latent content, the hidden or deeper meanings associated with the elements in an artefact.

Artefact analysis and the FraIM

It's now time to bring these three different methods of artefact analysis together in a more integrated and holistic approach that is the hallmark of the FraIM. Unlike other data collection procedures, you'll find that an integration of the different methods of artefact analysis relies on a more conceptual framing of these different approaches. This should not come as too much of a surprise because of the nature of the processes involved in the analysis and its overall purpose. The ultimate aim is to develop an understanding of the way we construct meaning out of our experiences through the analysis of social and cultural artefacts produced by people.

Figure 9.2 depicts an outline framework for how the three approaches contribute to this process of meaning-making and the nature of the other elements that impact on the process.

As you can see, the framework emphasises the inferential process of abduction. It shows that all artefacts are embedded in a particular discourse or discourse domain, which is located in one or more specific contexts. A domain is a sphere or area of cultural, social or intellectual activity that can give rise to the production of artefacts. Such artefacts have common characteristics that identify them as belonging to that particular domain. You'll remember from earlier sections of this chapter that artefacts can include texts, such as books and magazines, and performances such as theatre and dance. They can also make use of the senses of vision, sound, smell, taste and touch for their production and reception. A discourse domain, therefore, provides the source of the artefacts you are studying and partly determines their characteristics. Examples would be advertising, eco-tourism, economics, epistemology, radio news or the practice of vegetarianism.

Whatever the domain from which the artefacts are drawn, the analysis will take place in a particular context. The context will make a contribution to the level at which the analysis is undertaken and to the level of complexity. For example, analysing a current political crisis using an economics discourse with a group of primary school children will yield a different outcome compared to undertaking such an analysis in a post-graduate economics seminar. In both cases, the discourse would be firmly located in an economics domain but the detail and analytical sophistication (one would expect!) would be at a very different level, due to the context.

Whatever the domain, the process of semeiosis, mentioned earlier, will result in the production of artefacts constructed from signs taken from that particular discourse domain. This will allow participants in this process to gain access to the codification of selected knowledge and understanding based on the combination of signs drawn from the particular discourse domain.

An artefact, therefore, is a means of encoding and expressing information, knowledge and understanding, in order to make these accessible to and usable by the participants involved in the process. It does this through drawing on the range of different codes to which we have access as members of particular groups, communities and societies. It functions through informing, presenting, re-presenting and interpreting the information, knowledge and understanding about the issue under study.

The task of artefact analysis involves either the pre-coding and/or the post-coding of an analysis of the signs from which the artefact is constructed. As you will know by now, pre-coded information involves the collection of numerical

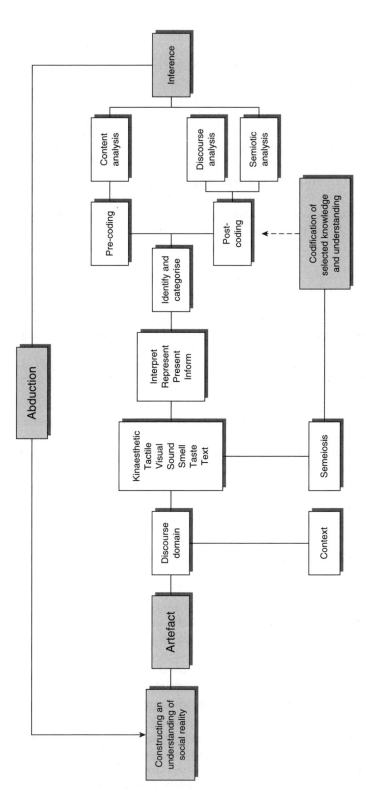

Figure 9.2 Abductive inference and artefact analysis

data and post-coding of information usually provides you with narrative data. Content analysis employs procedures that support the pre-coding of information before the data collection starts while semiotics and discourse analysis require you to code the data *after* they have been collected.

Analysis of an artefact will, therefore, enable you to draw on your understanding of the way that information, knowledge and understanding are encoded through the production of artefacts. You will then be able to use that insight to inform the analytical, deconstruction process of de-coding during analysis.

Drawing on the methods of content analysis, discourse analysis and semiotic analysis will, therefore, enable you, as the researcher, to understand more fully the selected aspect of the social reality you have chosen to study. It will enable you to do this through the inferential process of *abduction*.

Summary 9.2

- Artefacts are always embedded in a particular discourse domain, located within a specific context, which influences the selection and combination of signs.
- Signs become meaningful through the process of semeiosis or signification.
- Artefacts function by drawing on a range of different codes, or systems of rules, or discourses.
- Artefact analysis aims to identify and categorise the signs of the artefact by employing methodological procedures of pre-coding or post-coding of information.
- This is achieved through using content analysis, discourse analysis or semiotic analysis.

Inference and abduction

The idea of abductive inference or abductive reasoning comes from the semiotics of Peirce, who stated that:

> The surprising fact C is observed,
> But if A were true, C would be a matter of course;
> Hence there is reason to suspect that A is true. (1934: 117)

To put this more simply, abduction is concerned with arriving at an explanation, or the best available hypothesis, for an event that has already taken place. Originally, it was put in terms of developing and forming an explanatory hypothesis to help understand the causes of an observed phenomenon (Fann, 1970). However, for purposes of this chapter, the important point about abductive inference is that it is a 'retroductive' process (Blaikie, 2000: 109). Retroductive means looking to the past in order to develop an explanation for an event in the present. It enables the researcher to provide an explanation, theory or hypothesis to explain regularities or recurring patterns in whatever is being studied.

Another way of putting this is to state that inferential reasoning and the process of abduction enable the researcher to provide an explanation of the way that knowledge and understanding of the phenomenon have been *codified*. The process of codification is based on rules that determine the different combination and organisation of signs that are embedded in a particular discourse. The rules or codes give meaning to our experiences and the artefacts that are created by those experiences.

As a result of carrying out an analysis of, for example, a written text, a radio programme or a theatrical performance, you will be in a position to make inferences about the underlying social structures and relations that have given rise to the artefact. Such structures and relations are expressed through the artefact and contribute to the construction of the artefact's meaning.

Basing research on the FraIM allows the researcher to draw on the different theoretical perspectives and activities outlined so far in this chapter. An example will illustrate how these perspectives might be integrated to gain maximum understanding and knowledge about a selected issue. It will demonstrate the applicability of using the FraIM to carry out research using artefact analysis.

Summary 9.3

- Abduction is a retroductive process which looks to the past to develop an explanation for an event in the present.
- Abductive inference leads to an explanation of the way that knowledge and understanding have been codified.
- Codification is based on rules that determine the different combination and organisation of signs that are embedded in a particular discourse.
- The rules or codes give meaning to our experiences and the artefacts that are created by those experiences.
- Artefact analysis enables abductive inferences to be made about how our understanding of social issues is constructed through the nature of the artefacts we are studying.

An example of integration

The following comments are based on an organisation called MozVolunteers, located in Zavora, Mozambique, which organises community and medical volunteer projects. The latter can be undertaken as an elective option as part of a degree in medicine. At the time of writing, opportunities include working for Doctors for Life, a charitable NGO (non-governmental organisation) local to the area. Volunteers can become involved in the following activities:

- patient contact and clinic work
- health education

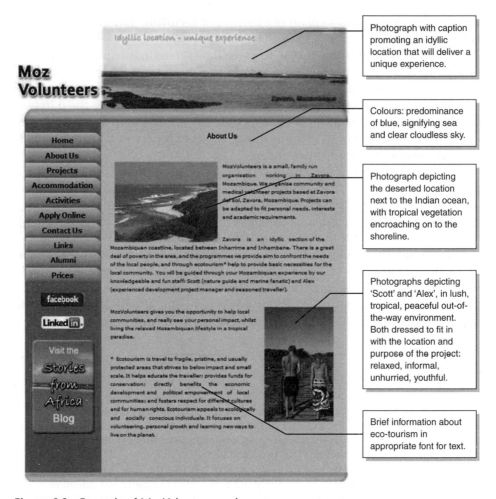

Figure 9.3   Example of MozVolunteers web page

- counselling
- HIV/AIDS
- malaria prevention and treatment
- home-based care in the rural area of Zavora.

MozVolunteers is run by two people, Alex and Scott. They have kindly given permission to refer to their organisation and their website for purposes of this chapter. Figure 9.3 depicts a page from the website. This provides an indication of the design and style of the site as well as the aims and purpose of the organisation. The web page in Figure 9.3 is in black and white although pages from the actual website are in full colour and, at the time of writing, can be accessed at www.mozvolunteers.com.

A detailed analysis of the web pages will involve moving from a basic level of description to a more sophisticated and challenging deconstruction of the ideological and political issues that are at play around such an organisation and its activities. The analysis is structured by the four functions of an artefact that were briefly outlined earlier in this chapter and can be approached as four stages of analysis. The higher the stage of analysis, the more sophisticated the process of deconstruction. However, you should bear in mind, of course, that the stages explain the theoretical levels of the deconstruction process and you would not necessarily follow each stage chronologically.

Stage 1: informational function of the artefact

The first stage is an important starting point for an analysis of the artefact. It involves being aware that the web pages exist and what they contain, since, as you will remember from Chapter 8, the function of this stage is to hold or store information.

Stage 2: presentational function of the artefact

The next stage entails identifying and categorising the linguistic and visual signs that make up the web pages on the site. This might also involve comparing the site with other similar sites, and could include a content analysis of the vocabulary, colours, illustrations, photographs, styles of writing and even such detail as the number of figures depicted in the sites. The information would be pre-structured and pre-coded, using a coding schedule that allows the collection of numerical data, through counting the elements or signs present.

An alternative approach would be to use a less structured method that draws on an understanding of the discourses referred to in the web pages. For example, it is clear that tourism, voluntourism, volunteerism and eco-tourism provide the discourses from which the signs of the page are drawn. There is also the discourse of 'getting away from it all' living a 'relaxed … lifestyle in a tropical paradise'. The attractions of experiencing such an exotic lifestyle are also reflected in the photographs: the deserted beaches, white surf of the warm ocean against a backdrop of a cloudless African sky. The page presents an attractive lifestyle that also provides opportunities for 'confronting the needs of the local people and through ecotourism help to provide basic necessities for the local community'.

The analysis relies on making sense of the collected data through the post-structuring and the post-coding of the information. It offers a description of the web page that draws on an understanding of the linguistic and visual discourses at play in this particular type of context. Analysis will result in narrative data that draw attention to the ideas presented in the page and will also allow progression to a deeper level of analysis.

Stage 3: representational function of the artefact

The representational function of an artefact goes beyond mere presentation to re-presenting ideas, information, knowledge and understanding about particular issues. Please remember, however, that these stages are more like points on a continuum. Analysis moves backwards and forwards along the dimension, drawing on discourses located in a particular context.

In the example here, the ideas the web page represent are about the enjoyment of doing something different and exotic. At the same time, the activities are worthwhile and of benefit to other people who are disadvantaged economically and socially. It is guilt-free tourism. Taking part will make a difference to the lives of the people in the locality and will contribute to the sustainability of the area depicted in the pages. The visual images describe an attractive and inviting environment where relaxation and hedonistic enjoyment are within a short walk. However, the text mitigates against any selfish or exploitative actions that staying here might lead to. Far from it: the visit of the eco-tourist 'benefits the economic development and political empowerment of local communities and fosters respect for different cultures and for human rights'.

MozVolunteers offers an eco-friendly experience while contributing to the sustainability of the local community. There are opportunities to work with the poor and look after disadvantaged children in the local community. It is not just selfish tourism. Volunteers with medical expertise can work with Doctors for Life at a newly built community clinic. Other opportunities include working on building projects, well-digging, creating vegetable gardens and developing irrigation systems, working with orphans and at crèches, providing admin help at the Doctors for Life clinic and becoming involved in malaria education, action and prevention. It is promoted as an idyllic, life-changing, authentic African experience, located in paradise in a remote area and off the beaten track overlooking the Indian Ocean.

Stage 4: interpretational function of the artefact

A more critical view would show that the web pages of MozVolunteers promote an attractive interpretation of an impoverished way of life. There is a strange juxtaposition of poverty and the lush physical environment that draws on our stereotypical view of an enjoyable and relaxing beach holiday away from the stress and strains of modern-day living. Fishing, sailing, scuba diving, surfing, snorkelling, kayaking and dining by lamplight are all organised by the staff of MozVolunteers while living the relaxed Mozambiquan lifestyle.

It is a cheap beach holiday that relies on exploiting the guilt feelings of the volunteers and takes advantage of the local community who are in need of assistance. It draws on images of Africans in poverty, living a life that is attractive to westerners – at least for a period of a few weeks. Then it's time to travel back home. Volunteers, it is stated, will have undergone personal growth and will take back with them an understanding of new ways of living on the planet. But what of the local community they will have left behind? How sustainable will their lifestyle be? How much real improvement will they have experienced as a result of the involvement of the volunteers?

You may feel that this is a rather cynical and unfair analysis of the work that MozVolunteers is doing. After all, they are recruiting volunteer medical staff for a brand new clinic and volunteers who will work in the community with disadvantaged children and adults. But remember: this approach to research invites you to take a *critical* perspective that attempts to look at the underlying ideologies that are the basis of the ideas in a document, text or other type of artefact you are studying.

It is a useful method of data collection and analysis when you are confronted with cultural and social artefacts that draw on a range of powerful institutional discourses, and are created using a persuasive and all-pervasive process of connotative semeiosis. It will enable you to develop an awareness of how meanings are created and what those meanings imply for the way we relate to each other, and the perspectives we are encouraged and expected to take on important issues.

Artefacts that function at the interpretational level present and continually re-present those interpretations through the commonly and intuitively understood symbols, signs and discourses of the societies in which we live. The analysis uses the process of abductive reasoning and inference to develop a critical and iterative understanding of the social reality within which we are immersed.

Conclusion

Chapters 8 and 9 have provided an insight into a method of data collection that is complex and sophisticated. The method, artefact analysis, provides a way of understanding the cultural and social characteristics of the world(s) we inhabit. These characteristics are at the very heart of the way we think, behave and relate to each other. They are about power and control, about ideology and about the all-pervasiveness of a hegemonic culture that determines in a very real way how we experience the world around us and how we construct our understanding of that world.

When you employ artefact analysis in your research, it is not an exaggeration to claim that the understanding you develop puts you in a privileged position. You will be able to use the insights you have developed to see through the superficial façade that so many come to accept as natural, real and legitimate but which is in fact constructed, discriminatory and oppressive. In the paraphrased and well-known words of the Zen master:

> To begin with, mountains are mountains and rivers are rivers. When we develop an insight into the truth, mountains are rivers and rivers are mountains. Eventually, further insight means that mountains again are mountains and rivers are rivers.

Your understanding allows you an insight that others will not have. However, such understanding will enable you to help others to develop that same degree of awareness of the social structures and relations that are an intricate and integral part of who we are and how we live our lives.

The three approaches that have been discussed in this chapter are usually treated as separate approaches to studying cultural and social artefacts. Employing an integrated strategy for your research will have shown you that it is possible, indeed it is almost unavoidable, to integrate the underlying principles on which the approaches are based. The FraIM encourages you to see artefact analysis as employing a broad, integrated strategy that draws on different methods. How exactly you approach this, of course, will be determined by the types of questions you ask in your research.

Reflections

1   How can you include artefact analysis in your own research?
2   What artefacts would you consider including as the basis of the analysis in your research?
3   Which procedures would you use: content analysis, discourse analysis, semiotic analysis or a combination?
4   Apply the framework from Figure 9.2 to your approach.
5   Discuss whether or not you find this framework helpful.

Associated reading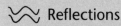

- Deacon, D., Pickering, M., Golding, P. and Murdock, G. (2007) *Researching Communications* (2nd edn). London: Hodder Arnold. See Chapter 6, 'Counting contents'.
- Fann, K. T. (1970) *Peirce's Theory of Abduction*. Martinus Nijhoff: The Hague.
- Hall, S. (2001) 'Foucault: Power, Knowledge and Discourse', in M. Wetherell, S. Taylor and S. J. Yates (eds), *Discourse Theory and Practice: A Reader*. London: SAGE.
- Hodson, R. (1999) *Analyzing Documentary Accounts*. London: SAGE.
- Hudson, P. (2005) 'Numbers and words: quantitative methods for scholars of texts'. See Chapter 8 in G. Griffin (ed.) *Research Methods for English Studies*. Edinburgh: Edinburgh University Press.
- Krippendorff, K. (2004) *Content Analysis: An Introduction to its Methodology* (2nd edn). London: SAGE.
- Neuendorf, K.A. (2002) *The Content Analysis Guidebook*. London: SAGE.

10

Data integration

> **This chapter will:**
>
> - identify the two types of data usually associated with undertaking research
> - help you become aware of the different levels of data used in research
> - show you how to integrate the different types of data through data transformation
> - enable you to apply the process of data transformation to your own research.

Introduction

This chapter is about the types of data you will work with in your research. The chapter takes a fresh view of what data are and how they can be used. A quick aside: please note that the word 'data' is plural. You should always write 'data are' or for example 'the data were collected' and not 'was collected'.

The chapter argues that, for a lot of the time, different types of data are automatically integrated without us even being aware that this is what we are doing. It's a natural part of the data processing activity. However, in this chapter you will not read about analysing numerical data using statistics or analysing narrative data using, for example, grounded theory. Such information is readily available in a variety of methodology textbooks and a number of selected titles are included in the 'Associated reading' section at the end of the chapter. What you *will* read about is a fresh view of data and their use. It will be a different view, a re-view, of how you might think about data and what data are.

Two types of data?

It is usually argued that there are two types of data. The FraIM refers to these as numerical and narrative data. This basic distinction is between, on the one hand, numbers, and on the other, words and everything else (Blaxter, Hughes and Tight, 2006).

The former are concerned with procedures based on counting and/or measuring. This type of data is often seen as relatively unambiguous, fixed and drawing on the use of the logical code and accepted conventions of mathematics (Guiraud, 1975) or scientific code (Chandler, 2001). Numerical data employ the logical rules and operations of addition, subtraction, multiplication and division.

Narrative data, on the other hand, deal with words and other types of texts, for example, still and moving images and audio texts. The data are very often ambiguous. They have meanings that are not fixed but are fluid. The meanings are often contentious, with relatively more opportunities for different interpretations. The data draw on conventional codes of meaning that are based on the use of language or visual or auditory imagery, with all their associated complexities, ambiguities and uncertainties. The meanings of the data are more open to negotiation and draw more closely on the subjectivity and interpretations of the researcher.

Each type of data has further characteristics that will be explained in more detail later. You will find that each has advantages and disadvantages and different functions and purposes. As you plan your research, you will need to consider what type of data you will collect. Of course, you will not be too surprised to discover that when using an integrated methodology approach, it is legitimate to collect *both* types of data.

A traditional approach to undertaking research makes great play of the differences between narrative and numerical data. But Halfpenny argues that 'despite obvious surface differences between words and numbers [such] data are not fundamentally different' (1997: 6). This may seem a rather unusual claim to make but, on reflection, you'll find there is some truth in this.

All data, whether numerical or narrative, result from the intervention of the researcher in that part of the social world that is chosen for study. The researcher structures, to a greater or lesser extent, the information that is generated. This process involves systematically coding information into data that can be manipulated to generate meaning or impose order and control, and sometimes predictability, on the small slice of the world under study. This is achieved using numbers, words and/or other types of imagery, such as photographs, drawings or sounds.

After the data have been collected you will need to decide how the data will be analysed. If you take a relatively traditional approach to research, you would probably be looking forward to using mathematical and statistical analyses for numerical data and an appropriate analysis for narrative data. However, from what has been written so far, it will be clear that there is no need to restrict yourself to such a limiting and limited strategy. There are other ways to approach this. You may want to turn your narrative data into numerical information or describe your numerical data with the use of written text. This can be represented in the choices listed below.

Choice 1

Numerical data are analysed mathematically to produce frequencies, based on statistical analyses. For example, research involving control and experimental groups might produce different scores on a particular ability. The arithmetical mean or other statistics can be calculated to measure the difference between the groups' scores. The results are then presented in tabular form.

Choice 2

Narrative data are analysed to produce counts, frequencies and percentages. For example, the number of times a particular category of word is mentioned in a chapter in a textbook. Another example would be counting the number of times young people's attitudes to work experience are mentioned in transcriptions of interviews with employers.

Choice 3

The third choice may involve producing written descriptions and explanations of the numerical information in your data. For example, you would produce a written account that describes and explains the numerical results from the survey mentioned in Choice 1. The words would function to *anchor* (Barthes, 1993) the meaning of the findings.

Choice 4

Here, written analyses and descriptions of narrative data are produced to identify, describe and explain the salient features and ideas present in the artefact.

Levels and types of data

It is generally accepted that there are four levels of data: nominal, ordinal, interval and ratio. This classification was first put forward by Stevens only as recently as 1946. Usually, these levels are only discussed in relation to *numerical* data. The levels are seen as a hierarchy of data, with ratio data being the most desirable level to aim for. In mathematical and statistical terms, this is a legitimate aspiration. However, in relation to carrying out social and educational research, this has the effect of privileging numerical data over narrative data. This is a position, of course, that is untenable when using an integrated methodology. The FraIM treats all methods – and data – as being equally acceptable and their use is determined predominantly by the research question and the aims and purpose of the research.

For the rest of this chapter, therefore, when levels of data are referred to, this should not be taken to mean that the higher levels are necessarily more desirable than the lower levels. They are only more desirable if the research question warrants, or justifies, their use.

Types of data

It is useful to be aware of the relationship between *levels* of data and the two *types* of data.

Narrative data are collected at the nominal and ordinal levels and numerical data at the interval and ratio levels.

Nominal level of data

The word nominal means name or naming. At this level of data all we can do is put a name or label to the variables or phenomena under study. Nominal data provide a categorisation or classification of information. Examples would be gender, or perhaps different types of fruit, say apples, bananas, oranges and pears.

Using the example of fruit, your research might involve writing an account about someone's diet consisting of a variety of different types of fruit. At the nominal level of data, it is unlikely that you would need to use the labels 1 to 4: there would be no need.

As you know, you can analyse photographs as part of your research. The analysis may include identifying individual elements that signify important cultural information. For example, the images may indicate the social background of the people depicted in the scene or there may be gendered issues presented through the images. Here, you would be dealing with nominal data and your research report would include descriptive accounts or narratives.

Ordinal level of data

Ordinal data not only provide a categorisation or classification of information but also allow the categories to be placed in rank order. An example would be the hierarchy for the armed forces, where the rank of private might be given 1; lance corporal 2; corporal 3; sergeant 4; staff sergeant 5 and sergeant major 6.

You will no doubt have already come across one very common form of ordinal data. These are often found in questionnaire surveys where you are invited to indicate on a five-point scale how strongly you agree or disagree with a statement. You might also have used such an approach in your own previous research.

The underlying principle of using a five-point scale comes from the well-known Likert (1932) scale, which you will also be able to read about in Oppenheim (2000). The important word here is 'scale', which suggests a dimension or continuum containing either discrete steps or continuous gradations that progress through different levels.

At first sight, the dimension of strongly agree through to strongly disagree in the questionnaire survey mentioned above consists of a clear and straightforward continuum with five unique points. Very often the next stage in this process is to record respondents' scores and then to calculate the arithmetic mean for each item for the whole sample. For example, if there were a sample of 100 participants, their responses would vary between 1 and 5 for an item. Totalling all the individual scores and dividing by 100 would result in a mean score for the item. This could then be used for comparison purposes either over time or between different groups and individuals responding to that item when completing the same questionnaire.

For example, let's say the mean score for the item is 3.6. If an individual circled the figure 2, that is, 'Agree', for this item then this response would be below average for the group of 100 participants who completed the questionnaire. However, it is arguable whether or not it is legitimate to subject ordinal data to mathematical calculations in this way. That's because we are dealing with *narrative* data and not *numerical* data.

You may want to ask yourself, therefore, if there really is a continuous scale, ranging from 'strongly agree' to 'strongly disagree'? How can we know that the differences between 'strongly agree' and 'agree' and between that of 'strongly disagree' and 'disagree' are the same? It is highly likely that each point on the dimension represents an interpretive difference in feeling, attitude and experiential value of the issue under study. In other words, *my* 'agree' may not mean the same as *your* 'agree' when we both respond to the same item on the questionnaire. The same can also be applied to scales that *appear* more obviously to be continuous, like the example in Table 10.1.

Table 10.1   Using a 'continuous' scale

For each of the following items, place a cross on that part of the scale which represents your view.		
Eating meat is morally defensible	··**x**·····	Eating meat is morally indefensible
It is acceptable to eat any kind of fish	···················**x**·······································	It is unacceptable to eat any kind of fish
It is acceptable to eat animal products	·········**x**··	It is unacceptable to eat animal products
We should grow GM crops	···**x**·········	We should ban GM crops

Again, however, it is doubtful that the scales in Table 10.1 represent true *numerical* dimensions on which the judgements lie. The dimensions represent a way of comparing experiences through a descriptive, experiential process that changes from one extreme to its opposite. In other words, the point that is being made in this section is that when it comes to ordinal level of data, strictly speaking, we are dealing with narrative and not numerical data.

We order the data by allocating a number to the categories or variables. This indicates a progression along a dimension. Alternatively, we might also want to describe the progression by using words such as 'more' or 'less', 'smaller' or 'larger', but without assigning a numerical value to the descriptions. If you want to work with numerical values, then you will need to be working with the next two levels of data: interval and ratio data.

Interval data

Interval data also classify/categorise and order information but with the addition of a further characteristic: the ordering has equal intervals between points on a scale. In educational and social research there are very few interval scales as such. The two most common general examples are first, time measured in calendar years, and, second, temperature recorded in degrees Celsius or Fahrenheit.

The time between years is identical, as is the step in temperature recorded by a thermometer. For example, the difference between 15 and 30 degrees Celsius is the same as the difference between 25 and 40 degrees Celsius. In fact, interval data are the first numerical data you will encounter on the list of data types. It means that the data can be subjected to mathematical operations such as addition and subtraction. In other words, the *numerical value* of the numbers can be used in an analysis and description of the information provided by such data.

Ratio data

What interval data do not have, however, is a *true zero value*. Only ratio data have such a zero point on their scales. This allows more precise and useful comparisons to be made between variables. Examples would include mass and length. Scores on a mathematical test would also fit this level of data as would, for example, the number of times a particular location is visited by a sample of students over a stated period of time. So, ratio data have all the characteristics of the three preceding levels, but with the additional property of having a true zero point.

Returning to the interval scale of temperature, the Celsius scale does of course have a zero point, but this is arbitrary. It is set at the condition where water turns to ice at normal atmospheric pressure. However, temperature recorded in degrees Kelvin *does* have a true zero point, which is the equivalent of -273 degrees centigrade. Nothing can fall below this temperature and so is considered to be a temperature of absolute zero. It would not be correct to claim that 30 degrees centigrade is three times the temperature of 10 degrees centigrade. However, it *would* be correct to say that, for example, 200 degrees Kelvin is twice that of 100 degrees Kelvin.

Table 10.2 summarises the differences between the four different levels of data and their association with the two different types of data.

Table 10.2 Summary of differences between levels and types of data

Type of data	Level of data	Categorical identification of item	Rank/ordered position	Equal intervals between points on the scale	True zero point
		Characteristics of data			
Narrative	Nominal	✓			
	Ordinal	✓	✓		
Numerical	Interval	✓	✓	✓	
	Ratio	✓	✓	✓	✓

Illustrative example of data levels

Table 10.3 provides examples and further details of the four different levels of data measurement and the criteria and conditions that help define the different levels. The examples are based on an imagined research project that aims to investigate food consumption in schools. Interval and ratio data have been combined into one category, due to the limited examples of interval data that are used in educational and social research, as already mentioned.

Food consumption: nominal level of data

As you can see from Table 10.3, at the nominal level, we would be studying the variable 'types of food eaten at school lunchtime'. The method of data collection would probably be observation, although as an alternative, the researcher might ask pupils to complete a questionnaire about the types of food they eat.

The aim of the data collection at the nominal level would be to identify and describe the types of food that pupils eat at lunchtime. This would result in either a list or a more lengthy narrative description and discussion of the types of food identified. Numbers can be assigned to each of the types of food eaten. The numbers might be used, for example, on the check-out till as pupils pay for the food. Rather than a number, however, a photograph of the food could be used just as effectively, since the data are at the nominal level.

Depending on the overall aims of the research, it may not be necessary to allocate a number to the types of food. It may be more appropriate to present the information as a narrative. Indeed, it hardly needs stating that research reports are primarily based on narrative accounts that can be highly sophisticated and discuss quite complex issues that have no need of any type of number.

Food consumption: ordinal level of data

At the ordinal level we can add information to the categories we have identified. As shown in Table 10.3, the variable under study might be, for example,

Table 10.3 Illustrative example of data levels: food consumption

Type of data	Narrative data		Numerical data
Level of data	**Nominal**	**Ordinal**	**Interval/ratio**
Description of levels of data	Nominal data provide an opportunity to classify, identify and label information.	Classify and order/rank information.	**Interval:** Classify and order/rank information with equal intervals between points on a scale with an arbitrary zero. **Ratio:** Classify and order/rank information with equal intervals between points on a scale with a true zero.
Variable or issue	1 Types of food eaten at school lunchtime.	2 Pupils' attitudes to healthy eating.	3 The number of items of food eaten by each of 10 pupils over a full week. 4 The amount of time pupils spend in the dining hall.
Type of variable	Nominal variables	Ordinal variables	Discrete numerical or continuous numerical
Characteristics of data	Categorising	Ordering	Counting or Measuring
Aims of data collection	1 To identify different types of food eaten.	2 To survey pupil attitudes to healthy eating.	3 To count the different types of foods eaten. 4 To measure time spent in the dining hall.
Method of data collection	1 Observation of types of food eaten.	2 Questionnaire survey of pupils' attitudes to healthy eating.	3 Observation/questionnaire of different types of food eaten. 4 Observation of amount of time spent in dining hall at lunchtime.

Table 10.4 Attitudes to healthy eating

Statement	Strongly agree	Agree	Unsure	Disagree	Strongly disagree
	Please circle one number only for each statement.				
1 Fruit should be eaten as part of a healthy diet.	1	2	3	4	5
2 You should always have a glass of milk as part of your daily diet.	1	2	3	4	5
3 Eating white bread is good for you.	1	2	3	4	5
4 Eating an apple every day is a good idea.	1	2	3	4	5
5 It's OK to have fizzy drinks as long as they're diet drinks.	1	2	3	4	5

'pupils' attitudes to healthy eating'. The method of data collection could be a questionnaire. An extract from such a questionnaire might look something like Table 10.4.

As has already been pointed out, the responses from 1 to 5 in Table 10.4 should not, strictly speaking, be treated as a continuous interval or ratio scale.

Food consumption: interval/ratio level of data

At the interval/ratio level of data measurement, the data use the numerical value of the numbers associated with the variables. As you can see from Table 10.3, this would allow us to study variables such as 'the number of items of food eaten by each of 10 pupils over a full week' or 'the amount of time pupils spend in the dining hall'.

In order to address the first question, the research might employ either observation or a pupil questionnaire asking about the different types of food eaten over the chosen period of time. To answer the second question, the method of data collection would probably involve observation, possibly using an electronic recording system based on pupil swipe cards, where the system would record the amount of time between swiping in and swiping out of the dining hall on each visit. This might result in the findings depicted in Table 10.5.

Due to the level of data, it is now possible to carry out a range of calculations or operations on the data, such as the arithmetic mean, that use the numerical value of the numbers attached to the variable 'time spent in dining hall'.

Data transformation

So far, you have looked at a number of examples about the four different levels of data. The next stage in understanding how the different levels relate to each other is that of *data transformation*. This consists of data reduction and data enlargement.

Table 10.5   Question 1: time spent in school dining hall

Pupil	Time spent in dining hall at lunchtime
Pupil 1	12 minutes
Pupil 2	10 minutes
Pupil 3	22 minutes
Pupil 4	16 minutes
Pupil 5	26 minutes
Pupil 6	32 minutes
Pupil 7	30 minutes
Pupil 8	14 minutes
Pupil 9	11 minutes
Pupil 10	5 minutes
Total	**178 minutes**
Mean	**17.8 minutes**

Most textbooks on research methodology usually point out that data reduction from a higher to a lower level is permitted, but that it is *not* permissible to transform data from a lower to a higher level. However, undertaking research would be very limited and limiting if data transformation were not permissible in both directions! At first sight, this might appear to be an irreconcilable argument between researcher positions. However, it depends, as you can imagine, on how data transformation is defined and exactly what is involved in both data reduction and data enlargement.

When using the FraIM, data reduction is seen as the process whereby data from a higher level are processed to produce data at a lower level. Data enlargement, on the other hand, is the opposite. Here, though, *additional data* are needed in order to transform the data to the higher levels.

Data enlargement

Nominal to ordinal

Nominal data can be transformed into ordinal data by the addition of information aimed at ordering or ranking the original data. For example, imagine I have a small collection of films on my bookshelf. I can give you the titles, tell you who the starring performers are and also the names of the directors of each film. If you are *really* interested I could probably give you an outline of the plot of each of the films.

So far, this information falls into the nominal category of data. But it is fairly limited, especially if you want to know how the films compare with each other. Also, you may want to borrow a film so you would ask me what I would recommend. Fortunately, I have arranged the films on the shelf in order of entertainment value. I also keep a list of the films in a notebook and I have given the most entertaining film a number 1, the next number 2 and so on. I have now moved on to the next level of data, ordinal, which enables me to rank the films in order of interest. (By the way, this may seem rather a sad example of how someone might spend their time, but please bear in mind I don't actually have a numbered list of films, although the shelf of films is real!)

Nominal to interval/ratio

Nominal data can be transformed into interval/ratio data by the addition of units of counting or measurement to the nominal variables to create interval or ratio data. Discrete or continuous data can be generated by this process. Staying with the film example, in my notebook I may have a record of the duration of the films and the number of times I have watched each film. The former provides continuous data and the latter discrete data, both at the interval/ratio level.

Ordinal to interval/ratio

Ordinal data can be transformed into interval/ratio data by the addition of similar units of counting or measurement, as in the above example of transforming nominal to interval/ratio data. Again, this will create data that are either discrete or continuous. For example, I might associate the ranked films with different viewing frequencies and also of course with the amount of time I have spent watching the films. The higher the ranking, the higher the frequency and the greater the amount of time spent viewing the film.

Data reduction

Interval/ratio to ordinal

Interval/ratio data can be transformed into ordinal data by the process of data reduction. This can be achieved by grouping the data into ranges in order to create new categories that are ordered or ranked. For example, if the information I hold indicates how long each film lasts, the data are at ratio level.

However, I may be more interested in knowing which are the long films, over three hours in duration, which are the short films, of less than one and a half hours, and which films are in between. Once I divide up the films in this way, the data will have been reduced into three categories: long, medium and short films. Of course, the amount of information this provides is not as detailed as knowing exactly how long each film lasts.

Interval/ratio to nominal

Interval/ratio data can be transformed into nominal data by grouping data into descriptive categories. There is no attempt to place the categories in any order.

Imagine that I have now decided to arrange my films, not in entertainment value, but in genres. This will enable me to select a film to suit my mood. The genres I use to categorise the films would be, for example, adventure, crime, science fiction and thriller. These categories are not placed in any order of preference or level of interest. They are not based on any type of criteria that indicate that one is better than or has a higher ranking than any other. They are simply classified according to whether or not their characteristics fit the genre descriptions.

Again, the amount of information this new categorisation provides is not as detailed as knowing exactly how long each film lasts or whether a film falls into the short, medium or long ordinal category.

Ordinal to nominal

Transforming ordinal data into nominal data involves a similar process of grouping data into descriptive categories as in the above, where interval/ratio data were reduced to nominal data.

So, the films were acquired for their entertainment value. Initially, they were not organised in any way and simply piled on the bookshelf after viewing. However, as a result of the data collection procedures I can now organise the films in a number of different ways. They can be grouped according to genre, they can be grouped based on being long, medium or short in duration, and they can also be grouped according to the exact running time. Table 10.6 shows the final presentation of all three different levels of data and how they link together.

Table 10.6   Linking different levels of data

| Film number | Narrative data | | Numerical data |
	Nominal data	Ordinal data	Interval/ratio data
12	Adventure	3 Long	3hrs 6mins
6	Crime	3 Long	3hrs 30mins
1	Thriller	3 Long	3hrs 10mins
4	Adventure	2 Medium	2hrs 50mins
5	Science fiction	2 Medium	2hrs 36mins
7	Crime	2 Medium	2hrs 31mins
11	Science fiction	2 Medium	2hrs 24mins
8	Science fiction	2 Medium	2hrs 40mins
10	Crime	2 Medium	1hrs 38mins
9	Thriller	1 Short	1hrs 29mins
2	Adventure	1 Short	1hrs 27mins
3	Thriller	1 Short	1hrs 26mins

Summary 10.1

- Data transformation consists of data enlargement and data reduction.
- Data enlargement requires additional data to transform data to the higher levels.
- Data reduction is the process through which data from a higher level are processed to generate data at a lower level.
- Nominal data are transformed into ordinal data by the addition of information to order or rank the original data.
- Nominal and ordinal data are transformed into interval/ratio data by the addition of units of counting or measurement to the original nominal variables.
- Data reduction from interval/ratio to ordinal is achieved through grouping the original data into ranges to create new ordered or ranked categories.
- Data reduction from interval/ratio and ordinal to nominal is achieved through grouping data into descriptive variables that are not ordered or ranked.

Further issues

You will need to take into account two further, but related, issues when considering the type of data to collect. The first is the *precision* you want to provide about the issues you are studying. The second is the degree of *restriction* you are prepared to accept in the conditions for using and analysing the data.

Precision

As the data level increases, the description of the phenomena under study becomes more precise. For example, to know that a film lasts 1 hour 20 minutes is to be a lot more precise than saying that it is a short film. However, the descriptions are also more narrow in the amount of information that is provided. To describe a film as belonging to the thriller genre, immediately identifies it as having a range of certain characteristics in common with a good number of other similar films. This information is far richer in its meaning, implications and associations compared to saying that a film lasts 1 hour and 29 minutes.

Restriction

At the same time, conditions for the use and analysis of the data are far more restrictive as the level of data increases. For example, to be considered as ratio data, information is expected to meet all the criteria of the lower levels plus the presence of a real zero to the scale. Figure 10.1 indicates the relationship between the level of precision and the degree of restriction associated with these two data characteristics.

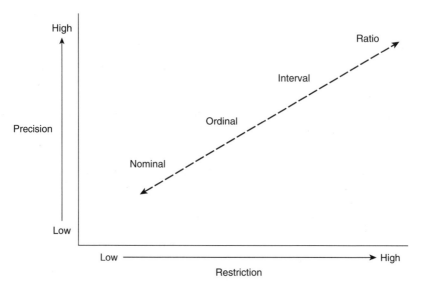

Figure 10.1 The relationship between the level of precision and the degree of restriction

Conclusion

Traditional thinking about data collection and data processing has a long history of a well-established polarisation between the two different types of data and how those data should be analysed. This chapter has tried to demonstrate that the differences are not as clear-cut as is usually argued. It is possible, indeed desirable, to integrate the different types of data through the dual processes of enlargement and reduction.

The next chapter looks at a very important, and challenging, issue: the warrantability of the research you undertake. This is about the use of data that provides the basis of the evidence you will use to make claims about your cases, which in turn will lead you to being able to arrive at valid and credible conclusions to your research. In other words, it is about answering the research question(s) you have set yourself at the outset of your research.

Reflections

1   What types of data are you planning to collect in your research?
2   To what kind of analysis will you subject the data?
3   All data start as narrative data. What is your view of this? Can you think of any examples where this does not apply?
4   To what extent will your research involve data transformation?
5   Whereabouts on the level of precision/degree of restriction graph will your data lie and how will this affect your management of processing the data?

Associated reading

- Boyle, D. (2000) *The Tyranny of Numbers*. London: HarperCollins.
- Bryman, A. and Cramer, D. (2009) *Quantitative Data Analysis with SPSS 14, 15 and 16: A Guide for Social Scientists*. London: Routledge.
- Charmaz, K. (2006) *Constructing Grounded Theory*. London: SAGE.
- Field, A. (2005) *Discovering Statistics Using SPSS* (2nd edn). London: SAGE.
- Holloway, I. and Freshwater, D. (2007) *Narrative Research in Nursing*. Oxford: Blackwell.
- Lyons, E. and Coyle, A. (eds) (2007) *Analysing Qualitative Data in Psychology*. London: SAGE.
- Muijs, D. (2004) *Doing Quantitative Research in Education with SPSS*. London: SAGE.
- Pell, A. and Fogelman, K. (2002) 'Analysing quantitative data'. Chapter 14 in M. Coleman and A.R.J. Briggs (eds), *Research Methods in Educational Leadership*. London: SAGE.
- Salkind, N.J. (2008) *Statistics for People Who (Think They) Hate Statistics* (3rd edn). London: SAGE.
- Silverman, D. (2006) *Interpreting Qualitative Data* (3rd edn). London: SAGE.
- Velleman, P.F. and Wilkinson, L. (1993) 'Nominal, ordinal, interval and ratio typologies are misleading', *The American Statistician*, 47 (1): 65–72.

11

Warrantable research: using the FraIM as a guide

> **This chapter will:**
>
> - challenge the use of a traditional paradigmatic explanation of the concept of validity in research
> - discuss further the importance of providing inferential explanations for the findings of your research
> - explain why it is important to make appropriate decisions at each stage of the FraIM in order to produce warrantable research
> - enable you to use an integrated methodology to undertake small scale warrantable research.

Introduction

This chapter is about an important methodological principle which is given a number of different terms. In your reading you will no doubt come across the concept of *validity*. It might be said that this is the ultimate aim of any research, whatever the approach, whatever the focus and whatever the methodology. However, usually – and traditionally – this concept is treated differently by different authors depending on which paradigmatic strategy the author is drawing.

A common view of validity is that it refers to the extent to which a method measures what it is supposed to measure (Muijs, 2004: 65). Bryman (2008: 152) lists a number of different types of validity:

- face validity
- predictive validity
- convergent validity
- concurrent validity
- construct validity.

Cohen, Manion and Morrison (2007: 105) refer to 18 different types of validity! These are listed as:

- content validity
- criterion-related validity
- construct validity
- internal validity
- external validity
- concurrent validity

- face validity
- jury validity
- predictive validity
- consequential validity
- systemic validity
- catalytic validity

- ecological validity
- cultural validity
- descriptive validity
- interpretive validity
- theoretical validity
- evaluative validity.

If you want to become a well-informed student of methodological validity then you could spend a happy hour or so reading through an explanation of the different types of validity from the above authors!

A traditional, *correspondence* view is that research is valid if it is a true account of the phenomenon that is being researched and reported. By correspondence it is meant that the account provides an explanation that corresponds to, or mirrors as closely as possible, the reality that is being described. Bush explains that: 'The concept of validity is used to judge whether the research accurately describes the phenomenon which it is intended to describe' (2002: 65). Another definition puts it this way: 'Validity, from a realist perspective, refers to the accuracy of a result. Does it "really" correspond to, or adequately capture, the actual state of affairs?' (Robson, 2002: 100). The realist perspective, with an emphasis on using the methodologies of the natural sciences, is revealed in the following:

> ... the aim of the research enterprise ... is to use a *procedurally* objective set of methods in order to gain an *ontologically* objective understanding of the events and objects we study. (Eisner, 1993: 51)

Ontology, briefly, is about reality and 'ontologically objective' in the above means that the reality we have come to understand through research corresponds to the ontology or reality that we set out to study.

An explanation for the application of validity to alternative approaches to research that challenge a methodology modelled on the natural sciences comes from Guba and Lincoln (1998). Emancipatory, interpretative research aims to support, enlighten and emancipate its participants from social, psychological and political ignorance and repression. They recommend using the term 'authenticity'. This consists of:

- *fairness*: equal consideration should be given to all the various perspectives of participants in the research
- *educative authenticity*: research is valid when individual respondents' understanding of other viewpoints is enhanced
- *catalytic authenticity*: research should stimulate activity and decision making
- *empowering*: research should empower participants to act (Guba and Lincoln, 1998: 213).

In mainstream mixed methods research, Onwuegbuzie and Johnson (2006) recommend using the term 'legitimation' to discuss the overall criteria of assessment of mixed research studies.

So, terms such as 'truth', 'authenticity', 'accuracy', 'correspondence', 'understanding' and now 'legitimation' have all been used to explain the concept and application of validity in research. Like other terms used in methodological arguments, they can, at the same time, be both very helpful but also problematic! The issue here is the paradigmatic perspectives on which the authors have drawn. However, as you know, an integrated approach to undertaking research challenges using a basic polarisation of the traditional paradigmatic strategies. Therefore, an insistence on privileging one term over another does not sit comfortably with using the FraIM.

It does acknowledge, nevertheless, that it is essential to design, plan and carry out research that will lead to credible and confident answers to the research questions. It also acknowledges that using one term signals an oversimplification of the purposes of research. The FraIM makes it clear that research is a *process* as well as a series of purposeful *activities*.

It has already been argued that the success of any research is primarily based on making claims about the cases, thus placing the researcher in a position to be able to answer the research question(s). The following examines this process in more detail. The explanation for how the FraIM deals with this issue is based on the idea of carrying out *warrantable* research.

Warrantable research based on argument

The following account is taken from Toulmin's *The Uses of Argument*, which was first published in 1958 and is the source that the FraIM draws on to explain the idea of warrantable research. Although Toulmin's focus is on the logic and analysis of arguments generally, the principles and approach he uses can be employed to inform our thinking about educational and social research. To start with, Toulmin raises the question:

> Supposing valid arguments can be cast in a geometrically tidy form, how does this help to make them any more cogent? (1958: 95)

Then, in a series of simple – but not simplistic – diagrams, he sets out a method of how arguments can be analysed. His account culminates in a final structure, with an illustrative example, which is presented in Figure 11.1. Numbers, not appearing in the original, have been added to each stage for clarity.

The argument in Figure 11.1 can therefore be read as:

> The claim that Harry is a British subject is supported by the data that Harry was born in Bermuda. The warrant for the claim comes from the fact that a man born in Bermuda will generally be a British subject, unless there are conditions that negate this claim, such as both his parents are aliens or he has become a naturalised

American. However, we would want to qualify the claim by saying that he is *presumably* or *probably* a British subject, because there may be information that we are unaware of, that may come to light after we have made the claim.

As Toulmin then adds: 'Finally, in case the warrant itself is challenged, its backing can be put in: this will record the terms and the dates of enactment of the Acts of Parliament and other legal provisions governing the nationality of persons born in the British colonies' (1958: 104–5). In other words, we can refer to background information which will strengthen and support the claim.

This is a fascinating, and very useful, way of looking at how the relationship between data and claims can be evaluated through using warrantable arguments. Applying this approach within the FraIM enables us to take a new perspective on the process of planning, designing and carrying out credible

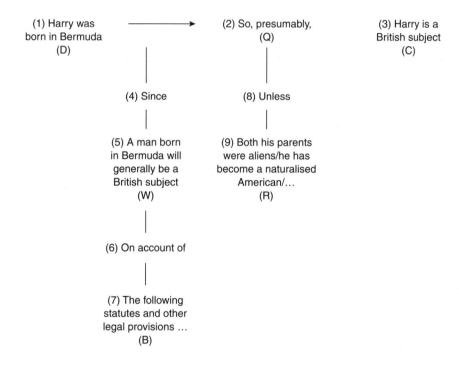

The letters stand for the following terms:

D = data
Q = qualifying condition, which acknowledges the possibility of a rebuttal or
      alternative explanation
C = claim
W = warrant
B = backing or support for the warrant
R = the rebuttal or alternative explanation

Figure 11.1   An illustration of the final structure of the argument
(*Source*: Toulmin, 1958. Numbers added.)

research. The next section looks at this in more detail and applies Toulmin's approach to educational and social research based on the FraIM.

Summary 11.1

- Traditionally, the concept of validity is treated differently depending on which paradigmatic strategy the research is based.
- Terms such as 'truth', 'authenticity', 'accuracy', 'correspondence', 'understanding' and 'legitimation' are used.
- The FraIM deals with validity through the use of the term 'warrantability of research'.
- The concept of warrantable research is based on Toulmin's (1958) *The Uses of Argument.*

Warrantable research and the FraIM

In any research, whatever the research question(s), we aim to make warrantable claims about the cases or the data sources. The claims are based on the evidence, selected from the data collected, using particular methods of data collection, drawing on identified data sources within a theoretical framework and particular contexts.

This procedure is aimed at enabling us to arrive at conclusions which provide answers to the research question(s). This whole process can be described as producing warrantable research. It involves providing the best available evidence to support the research claims and arriving logically at valid and true conclusions. In addition, it also includes considering, and subsequently rejecting, alternative explanations for the conclusions. Above all, it involves approaching the process in a *sceptical frame of mind.* As Gorard and Taylor point out:

> Consider any research claim (of ours or others), whether if that claim is not true, then how else could we explain the existence of the evidence leading to it? Only when all plausible alternative explanations, both methodological and substantive, have been shown to be inferior should the research claim be allowed to stand. (2004: 166/7)

Figure 11.2 presents the FraIM linked to Toulmin's approach to making warrantable claims.

As you can see, the basic structure is the FraIM with the addition of the warrant, qualifying conditions and backing conditions. The qualifying condition supplements the warrant and the backing conditions relate to the context, cases, methods and data, including data analysis. A brief example, using selected elements of the FraIM, will help to explain the addition of these components to the main FraIM and their contribution to producing warrantable research.

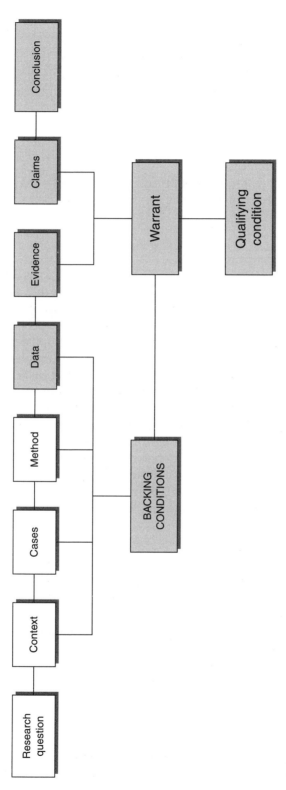

Figure 11.2 Warranting research and the FraIM

An example

Imagine you are interested in carrying out research into the amount of stress teachers are under and the emotional experience of undergoing an external school inspection. You intend to base your research on the following components of the FraIM.

Research question

Teachers undergoing external school inspection: to what extent is the level of self-reported stress associated with views about how useful the inspection process is?

Policy context

Ofsted (the Office for Standards in Education) is responsible for carrying out external inspections of the school system in England (UK). At the heart of the inspection process is a strongly held commitment that inspection should contribute to school improvement and raising standards of pupil achievement and attainment (Ofsted, 2004). The policy context, therefore, relates to the Ofsted inspection process and academic studies about its impact on schools. As far as the latter is concerned, there is some evidence that improvements resulting from inspection may only be cosmetic (Saunders, 1999) with schools 'papering over the cracks' and hiding the real issues during the time of the inspection visit (Plowright, 2007). Lonsdale and Parsons (1998) are just as sceptical, arguing that inspection disempowers teachers, polices the work carried out and creates an unsupportive and punitive culture. The process is seen as intrusive and threatening (Dean, 1995) so it will come as no surprise that many teachers find the experience highly stressful (Brimblecombe and Ormston, 1995).

Theoretical context

You have decided that the conceptual framework will draw on your understanding of the concept of the learning organisation (Pedler, Burgoyne and Boydell, 1991; Senge, 1990). You firmly believe that stress in the workplace can be mitigated by developing a supportive learning culture where learning creates positively valued outcomes (Huysman, 1999) and you will argue that this would be one way of managing the feelings of stress and threat experienced during inspection.

Cases

You intend to employ a combination of a case study and field experiment for the data source management. The case study school will be one that is undergoing or has undergone an external inspection in the previous three months. You will ask a number of teachers to take part in your research. Selection of the informants will be purposive, based on how stressful the teachers have felt the experience to be. You will compare a self-identified low stress group with a self-identified high stress group within the school.

Methods of data collection

You intend to use two methods of data collection. The first will be an initial questionnaire to determine which teachers fall into a high stress group and which fall into a low stress group. You will then interview teachers from each group. The purpose of the data collection is:

1 to explore teachers' views about how useful they found the inspection process
2 to determine if their views are associated with the level of stress they report experiencing during the inspection visit.

Data

The questionnaire will collect numerical data and the interviews will collect narrative data.

Claims and evidence

The data will enable you to make a number of claims about the informants who take part in the research, allowing you to draw inferences about the association between reported levels of stress and the usefulness of external inspection.

Conclusion

Let's assume that the conclusion of your research is that teachers who report experiencing a high level of stress find the external inspection process more useful than teachers who experience a low level of stress. This would be a very surprising conclusion!

Warrant

The warrant for your research will be based on the reasons you provide to explain this conclusion. Remember that this is based on the process of *inference*. This might involve arguing that those teachers who found the inspection visit more stressful were more concerned about reaching higher standards during the visit compared to their colleagues. They therefore found the inspection more useful because they were more concerned about:

- developing their professional practice
- learning how to improve their teaching
- being enthusiastic about sharing their understanding with colleagues in a supportive learning culture.

In other words, they were more concerned about reaching high standards during the inspection visit. Consequently, they succeeded in achieving higher standards and therefore found the visit more useful but, at the same time, more stressful.

Your inferential explanations will inevitably refer to the data you collected and will relate the analysis of teachers' comments to their views about the links between stress and external inspection.

Backing conditions

You will also refer, *explicitly*, to the policy and theoretical contexts of the research in order to back up and support your explanations or argument, that is, your *warrant* (or justification). In other words, you will be able to quote evidence from the published literature that supports your interpretation of the findings and the inferences you will make about the strength of the warrant to explain the findings. This literature will include the publications you referred to in the earlier context sections of your account.

Unlike some research approaches, explaining findings by drawing on warrantable evidence acknowledges the complexity of the research process. In particular, it treats the idea of cause and effect as being multifaceted and not a one-stage step that identifies a particular cause having a particular effect. This is a major problem associated with a traditional view of research based on the gold standard of experimentation. A true experiment employs one or more independent and dependent variables. It attempts to control extraneous variables that might interfere with identifying a causative link. Undertaking warrantable research using the FraIM argues that to understand the social and educational phenomena under study we need to consider the decisions that are taken *at each stage* of the research process. These include the range of contexts in which the research is embedded, the case selection strategy, the methods of data collection and the data and their analyses. Drawing on this framework enables you to make inferences about the relationship between the evidence generated and the claims, and subsequently the conclusions to the research.

If you have made *appropriate* decisions within each of these components of the FraIM, then you will be able to provide relatively *strong* warrants, or explanations or justifications, for your claims. If you have made *inappropriate* decisions at any stage, or provided insufficient information, then your argument will be *weakened*.

Qualifying condition

Remember that the qualifying condition Q, depicted in Figure 11.1, acknowledges that there may be the possibility of a rebuttal (R) of the explanations or warrant. Therefore, as Gorard and Taylor (2004) point out, research should always foster scepticism. This means not immediately accepting the explanation that you or others may offer for the findings. You should always consider alternative explanations and reasons for the results of your research. If one or more of these alternatives is more convincing and accurate, then it will have to be considered as a 'rebuttal' or a challenge to the initial explanation and the conclusion will need to be re-assessed. This is represented in Figure 11.3.

Rebuttal

The rebuttal involves challenging the explanation for the claims based on the findings. It may be a result of the erroneous inferences you have made about the evidence based on the data collected. It might also be a consequence of inappropriate decisions taken at any of the stages in the FraIM, as was mentioned above. Selected examples of what these might be are outlined, briefly, below.

Research question
The research question may be unclear and may not be related closely to the focus of the research. This may lead to inappropriate decisions later in the FraIM since it may lead to selecting an unhelpful sample, using inappropriate methods of data collection or collecting inappropriate data.

Context
The personal and professional context may be missing in your report or not described clearly and accurately. This may lead to an uncertainty about how to evaluate subsequent decisions reported in the research. For example, if the research was about the level of morale in an SME (small- and medium-sized enterprise) then it would help to know if the researcher was the proprietor/ managing director or an employee of the business. The reasons for undertaking the research, the types of questions asked and the interpretation of the findings would probably be influenced by who the researcher was.

In the example about teacher stress and the experience of undergoing an external school inspection, readers would need to know if, for example, the researcher was the head teacher or the school's union representative or a university researcher not connected to the school. The perspective and perception brought to the research may be very different depending on who is carrying out the research. This is in turn may have an impact on the inferential process of interpreting the findings.

Knowing something about the organisational context is also important for the readers of the research report. You would need to demonstrate that you have understood and explained clearly the nature and characteristics of the organisation in which you are conducting your research. This would need to include relevant and accurate information about size, general location, etc. In the above example, the findings resulting from studying teacher stress and inspection may be interpreted differently if the school is an all-boys, bi-lateral school of over

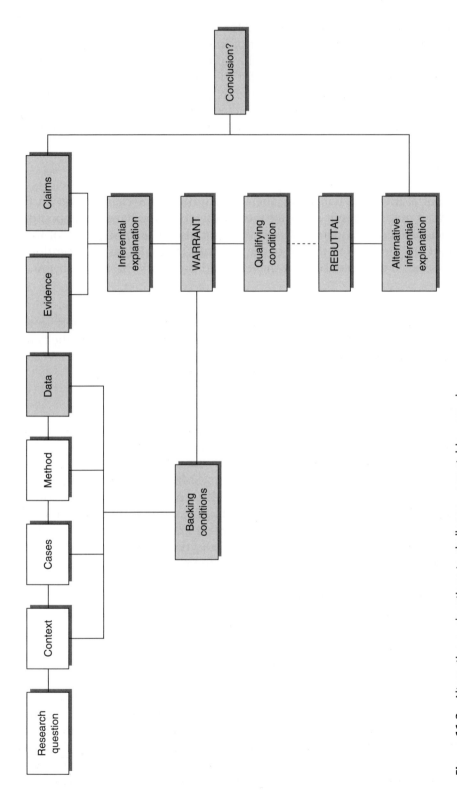

Figure 11.3 Alternative explanations to challenge warrantable research

1,300 pupils aged 11 to 18 years in an urban location, compared to a rural, mixed comprehensive school with only 500 pupils aged between 11 and 16 years.

Cases

If inappropriate decisions are made about the data source management and sampling strategy, then the data collected may not contribute to providing an accurate answer to the research question. To give an obvious example: if in studying teacher stress and inspection you interviewed parents and asked their views about the stress experienced by teachers in the research school, then you would not get a clear and accurate picture of the teachers' level of stress. Remember that the research question asks about the level of stress experienced by the teachers so interviewing parents would not be appropriate. When the teachers are interviewed, an appropriate sample would need to be selected and this selection process is crucial to the success of the research. For example, it is highly likely that only interviewing teachers from a particular department would give a skewed result of the experiences of the teachers in the school.

The sampling decision in this example would be aimed at choosing a purposive sample thus enabling us 'to choose a case because it illustrates some feature or process in which we are interested' (Silverman, 2006: 306). Here, this feature would be those teachers who, on the one hand exhibit particularly high levels of stress, and, on the other, those who show low levels of stress. Again, an inappropriate decision may lead to erroneous, misleading or incomplete results, so for example, if only teachers with high levels of stress were interviewed then the picture would be incomplete.

Methods of data collection

The choice of methods is based on degree of structure and level of mediation, as outlined in Chapter 5. In the example here, it would be more appropriate to use a highly structured method of asking questions rather than, say, examining school personnel documents using discourse or semiotic analysis or carrying out observations of the teachers. The choice of using a survey for the data source management with a written questionnaire would give the kind of information that provides a general overview of the teachers' perspectives of their experiences.

In addition, less structured interviews with selected teachers would be able to provide a detailed and in-depth insight into the emotional experience of the teachers as they underwent the inspection visit. If an inappropriate decision *had* been taken to, say, use observation then insufficient and probably inadequate data would be collected which would not be able to contribute successfully to answering the research question.

Data

Appropriate decisions have to be made about whether or not to collect numerical and/or narrative data, depending on the level of pre-structuring of the data demanded by the research. In the example above, it is important to discover the personal meanings that teachers construct about the inspection experience. Therefore, a highly structured questionnaire using closed questions that collected pre-structured data would not allow you to develop this depth of understanding. Collecting numerical data in these circumstances would not be an appropriate decision.

Data analysis

In addition, if you decide to use mathematical processing on your data, then you will need to ensure that the correct calculations are carried out and appropriate statistical testing is employed. Likewise, appropriate analysis of narrative data will need to be undertaken. As was pointed out in Chapter 10, data of whatever type can be analysed mathematically or narratively. For example, you may want to subject the narrative data collected during the interviews to a mathematical analysis to determine the number of times the idea of professionalism is mentioned by the teachers. This would be in addition to the narrative thematic analysis undertaken on the data.

Being aware of the above difficulties in the decision-making process at each stage of the FraIM will increase the likelihood of you being able to plan and carry out warrantable research. It will also enable you to question any research report you encounter, as long as sufficient information is provided about each stage of the research. If it is, then you will be in a position to question, challenge and criticise the research if you feel that inappropriate decisions have been made at any stage of the project.

Summary 11.2

- Toulmin's *The Uses of Argument* refers to: data, qualifying condition, claim, warrant, backing for the warrant, rebuttal/alternative explanations.
- Warranting research is based on the process of inference.
- Data, that are assumed to be true, lead to a claim which is supported by background information that provides a justification or warrant for the claim, unless additional information challenges the claim.
- Making appropriate decisions within each of the components of the FraIM will provide relatively strong warrants for your research.
- Making inappropriate decisions at any stage, or providing insufficient information, will weaken your warrant.

Conclusion

As a researcher, your main aim is to undertake warrantable research that results in valid conclusions that enable you to answer your research question(s). Using the FraIM makes the process clearer. It argues that the research is driven by the research question. It requires appropriate decisions to be made at each stage of the FraIM to ensure that the findings and conclusions are warranted, or justified. Such warrants or justifications are based on an inferential process. This process attempts to explain the claims in terms of the empirical evidence, that is selected from the analysis of the research data which are collected from the cases, using appropriate methods, and drawing on the supporting contextual factors underpinning the process.

The inferences provided will inevitably be open to question and therefore you should always take a sceptical and critical position to the interpretation of the findings. In addition, you should systematically consider alternative explanations based on counter-arguments for the warrants proposed. If the alternative explanations are *accepted*, or more convincing, then the conclusions can be queried and might well be rejected. If the alternative explanations are *rejected* then the warrant for the research survives as the best and most appropriate available at the time.

Finally, there can be some confusion about what exactly is being warranted or justified. You should remember that, ultimately, it is the actual *inferences* for which you will aim to provide justifications or warrants. If you achieve this, then you will have planned, designed and reported on carrying out warrantable research using the FraIM.

Reflections

1   Generally speaking, how will you ensure you produce warrantable research?
2   Consider in detail how you will make appropriate decisions at each stage of the research process, including:

- the research question
- contextual factors
- cases
- methods of data collection
- types of data
- data analysis
- claims and evidence
- conclusion.

3   As you write your research report, list what you consider to be the backing conditions, qualifying conditions and the potential rebuttals to your argument(s) as you think through how you can produce warrantable research.

Associated reading 📖

- Gorard, S. (2002) 'Fostering scepticism: the importance of warranting claims', *Evaluation and Research in Education*, 16 (3), 136–49.
- Gorard, S. and Taylor, C. (2004) *Combining Methods in Educational Research*. Maidenhead: Open University Press. See Chapter 10, 'Prospects for the "new" education and social science researcher'.
- Greene, J.C. and Caracelli, V.J. (2003) 'Making paradigmatic sense of mixed methods practice'. Chapter 3 in A. Tashakkori and C. Teddlie (eds), *Handbook of Mixed Methods in Social and Behavioral Research*. London: SAGE.
- Onwuegbuzie, A.J. and Johnson, R.B. (2006) 'The validity issue in mixed research', *Research in the Schools*, 13 (1), 48–63. Reproduced in V.L. Plano Clark and J. W. Creswell (eds) (2008), *The Mixed Methods Reader*. London: SAGE.
- Plantinga, A. (2008) 'Warrant: a first approximation'. Chapter 32 in E. Sosa, J. Kim, J. Fantl and M. McGrath (eds), *Epistemology: An Anthology* (2nd edn). London: Blackwell.
- Tashakkori, A. and Teddlie, C. (2008) 'Quality of inferences in mixed methods research: calling for an integrative framework'. Chapter 7 in M.M. Bergman (ed.), *Advances in Mixed Methods Research*. London: SAGE.

12

Ethical issues in participant-centred research

This chapter will:

- outline why ethics is important
- explain why researchers need to take ethics into account in their research
- identify the ethical issues that you will need to be aware of in relation to the participants in your research.

Introduction

Ethics is an important aspect of undertaking research and can, at times, be fraught with difficulties. You will have noticed that there are two chapters about ethics in this book. Most methodology texts focus exclusively on the experience of the *participants* in research and the decisions that researchers need to make to ensure their participants' well-being. This focus is covered in this first chapter about ethics, along with a brief look at the context of the ethical decisions you will be expected to take in your research. It examines why ethics is important, what ethics is about, why you should take ethics into account and the types of issues that you will need to be aware of in relation to the participants in your research.

However, there are other factors that, as a researcher, you should consider and these are discussed in Chapter 13, which offers a wider perspective. It highlights the issues associated with other stages in the FraIM and not just those associated with the research participants.

What is ethics?

A straightforward explanation of ethics is that it 'is concerned with respecting research participants throughout each project, partly by using agreed standards'

(Alderson and Morrow, 2004: 11). However, further reflection reveals that ethics is both an interesting term and a confusing one, as the following indicates:

> Ethics, the philosophical study of morality. The word is also commonly used inter-changeably with 'morality' to mean the subject matter of this study; and sometimes it is used more narrowly to mean the moral principles of a particular tradition, group or individual. (Audi, 1999: 284)

From this description, we can infer that ethics draws on:

1 *general* moral principles that determine attitudes, beliefs and relations between people
2 more *specific* moral principles that are associated with, say, a particular profession or a specific activity.

As will be discussed later in this chapter, specific moral principles associated with a profession have led to the proliferation of ethical procedures that are specific to that particular profession.

Rather than use the word 'ethics' it may be more appropriate to refer to *ethical behaviour* or *ethical practice*. This is because in research we are concerned with carrying out certain actions and activities and not just thinking about or theorising about the underpinning principles on which those actions are based. In the following sections, therefore, 'ethical behaviour' and 'ethical practice' are used interchangeably with the term 'ethics'.

One of the earliest, if not *the* earliest source of ethical concern appears to be the Hippocratic oath, written by the physician, Hippocrates, who lived in ancient Greece in the fourth and fifth centuries BC. It was a code of medical ethical behaviour that put the patient first. Rorty, Mills and Werhane point out that:

> The mainstay of professional ethics is the physician's commitment to the best interests of the patient. This Hippocratic tradition of medical ethics has influenced the professional codes of other health care workers, including nurses, hospital administrators and members of the allied health professions. (2007: 181)

Indeed, it appears to have laid the foundations for many of the ethical codes of practice in a variety of different professions with which we are now familiar. If you are interested in what the oath contains, then you might like to refer to Jacob's (1988) publication which prints it in full (it is not very long).

The concern for medical ethics and in particular the relationship between medical researchers and their 'subjects' took on an increased urgency as a result of the atrocities in the concentration camps of the Second World War. These were revealed in the Nuremberg trials where, in 1947, Nazi doctors were found guilty of conducting experiments on prisoners and were subsequently executed or imprisoned (Homan, 1991). As a direct consequences of such horrific events, the Nuremberg Code was produced. This is a set of 10 rules that should govern the conduct of research on humans, especially experimentation in medicine and psychology. The following is a shortened, paraphrased version, based on the full Nuremberg Code, cited in *British Medical Journal* (1996):

1   Participants should take part in the research on a voluntary basis.
2   The research is justified if it is the only way of generating the knowledge produced, which should be for the good of society.
3   The research should be justified by the anticipated results.
4   All unnecessary physical and mental suffering and injury should be avoided.
5   If death or disabling injury might occur then the research should not go ahead, except where the researchers also serve as subjects.
6   The degree of risk should never exceed the benefits of carrying out the research.
7   Participants should be protected from possibilities of injury, disability or death.
8   The research should be conducted only by qualified persons.
9   Participants should be free to end the research if they have reached the physical or mental state where continuation of the research appears impossible.
10 The research should be stopped if continuation is likely to result in injury, disability or death to the participant.

The Nuremberg Code has had far-reaching consequences for the way that social research is conducted. These include 'the development of ethical codes or guidelines, the quest for professional discipline, the establishment of ethics committees and the inclusion of ethics components in courses that prepare students for practice and research' (Homan, 1991: 15). However, there are examples of social research that have not followed codes of practice or guidelines and these highlight, some quite graphically, why researchers need to take ethical issues into account when planning and undertaking research.

Why researchers need to take ethics into account

One study from a number of years ago investigated the hypothesis that conversations between adults were less egocentric than children's conversations (Henle and Hubbell, 1938). The authors tested if adults used statements about themselves less often than children used such statements, hence the use of the term 'egocentric'.

You would think that from this brief description, the research would not appear to raise any potential ethical issues. However, your assessment will no doubt change when you discover that the data collection methods included the researchers hiding under the beds of students and making notes of their conversations! In addition, they eavesdropped on private discussions in social areas and listened to students' telephone conversations. This research raises important ethical questions, as do a number of now famous – or perhaps infamous – studies from not too long ago.

One of those studies is the series of experiments carried out in the 1960s by the psychologist, Stanley Milgram. It is worth describing this work in some detail. First of all, research subjects (as they were referred to in those days) were recruited to take part in a learning experiment 'on the grounds of an institution of unimpeachable reputation, Yale University' (Milgram, 1963: 377). On arrival at the university, they were shown to a human behaviour laboratory and introduced to a researcher in a grey laboratory coat. The technician's manner was impassive and stern throughout the proceedings. The task of the subject was to administer an electric shock to a learner strapped into a chair out of sight in the next room. The shocks were delivered through a sophisticated and impressive looking 'shock box' that was wired to the learner.

When the experiment began, the subject was instructed to administer an electric shock when the learner made an error while trying to learn word associations. On each incorrect response, the subject was instructed to increase the level of shock by pressing a switch on the shock box. All of the forty subjects who took part in the experiment increased the shock level to 300 volts.

Despite complaining about the effects the electric shocks would have on the learner and often being visibly distressed by the experiment, 26 subjects continued to the maximum level of 450 volts. This was beyond the level labelled 'Danger: Severe Shock'. Or so they thought. What was actually happening was that the learner, or *confederate*, was one of the researchers. No actual electric shocks were delivered. The learner's screams of pain and demands and pleadings to be let out of the room and for the experiment to be stopped were pre-recorded and were an integral part of the experiment.

The subjects in Milgram's research had been deceived into believing that the experiment was about learning. In fact, it was about obedience and authority. Two decades earlier, the world had seen Nazi Germany come to power and later witnessed the overwhelming suffering and devastation it had inflicted on the Jewish people through the concentration camps and gas chambers. Milgram's research was conducted with the laudable aim of drawing explicit parallels with those events. Or were the aims laudable?

The naïve subjects in this experiment suffered distress and anxiety. They were placed in an almost impossible situation that challenged their emotional and psychological well-being. They were deceived into carrying out what they thought were cruel actions against another human being. Ethically, the question still remains after many years: should these experiments have taken place? You might find it helpful to pause here and consider your own answers to this question.

Almost a decade later, another experiment was underway with equally serious ethical implications. This now famous – or again, perhaps infamous – experiment became known as the Stanford Prison Experiment (Haney, Banks and Zimbardo, 1973a; b; see also Zimbardo, 1973, and Zimbardo, 2007). This was a study of the psychological effects of prison life on prisoners and prison guards. In this case, however, the 'prisoners' and the 'guards' were student volunteers. The experiment involved a simulated prison environment where 21 male college students played the role of either prisoners or prison guards. Once the experiment was underway, the guards wore whistles around their necks and carried police batons. They had full responsibility for treating the prisoners in whatever way they wanted, within some limits. Events were regularly videotaped and conversations were secretly recorded. The prisoners wore identical tunics to each other, were known only by their identity numbers and were generally treated very badly, being verbally abused, humiliated and dehumanised. Meanwhile, the researchers stood by, carefully carrying out their observations, recording conversations and filming the behaviour of guards and prisoners. However, before too long, the experiment had to be terminated prematurely, after only six days, due to the impact it was having on the emotional well-being of the prisoners. For example:

> The most dramatic evidence of the impact of this situation upon the participants was seen in the gross reactions of five prisoners who had to be released because of extreme emotional depression, crying, rage and acute anxiety. (Haney, Banks and Zimbardo, 1973a: 10)

The 'pathology of power' was clearly being worked out in this experiment. Parallels were drawn between this simulation and the real world of the prison, but even now it still raises the question: is such an experiment ethically acceptable? Again, what is your own answer to this question?

The above, rather extreme, examples illustrate the kind of research that challenges both moral and ethical sensitivities in the way that participants are treated.

It was pointed out, at the beginning of this chapter that, usually, most textbooks highlight ethical problems from the perspectives of the people involved in the research. Ultimately, of course, it is indeed the people in the research that ethical decisions need to take into account. For example, Ritchie and Lewis (2003) list informed consent, anonymity, confidentiality and protecting participants and researchers from harm. Coolican also focuses on 'researchers' treatment of, and guarantees to, participants' (2004: 602). Cohen, Manion and Morrison (2007) include privacy, anonymity, confidentiality, betrayal and deception of the participants in research.

Hammersley and Traianou (2007) argue that there are five main ethical principles that are commonly recognised and that need to be taken into account when undertaking educational research. These are:

1   Harm: will the research cause harm to people?
2   Autonomy: can the participants decide for themselves whether or not to take part in the research?
3   Privacy: what information gathered from the participants will be made public?
4   Reciprocity: should participants expect anything in return from taking part in the research?
5   Equity: everyone involved in the research should be treated equally and no one unjustly favoured or discriminated against.

They make the point that very often these are in conflict with each other, so that for example:

in order to minimise potential harm to those we judge to be vulnerable, we may infringe their personal autonomy by insisting that others, those who know them well, must give permission on their behalf if they are to participate in a research project. Alternatively, if we insist that *they* have the sole right to make the decision about their participation, so as to respect their autonomy, we may be unwittingly subjecting them to risk of harm that could otherwise be avoided. The potential conflicts among this set of principles carries the implication that sometimes an action will be ethical in one respect and unethical in another. (Hammersley and Traianou, 2007)

Elliott refers to the importance of being aware of ethical and *political* issues when undertaking research. This distinction appears to be a useful one, since it draws attention to wider issues in research:

[T]he term 'ethical' is used to describe those issues that relate to the relationship between the researcher and the research subjects or participants, and the impact of the research process on those individuals directly involved in the research, while the term 'political' is used to describe the broader implications of research in terms of the impact it may have on society or on specific subgroups within society. (Elliott, 2005: 134)

This description is closer to the approach that the FraIM takes to ethics and is the focus of the next chapter. It acknowledges that ethical issues go beyond individual participants and that any research should take into account the wider moral and ethical implications of the research. Using the FraIM also provides a structure for considering these wider implications and as you will read in the next chapter, the focus is on *all* the different elements in the FraIM and not just on the participants in the research.

☐ Summary 12.1

- Ethics draws on two important factors:

  – general moral principles about attitudes, beliefs and interpersonal relations
  – specific moral principles associated with a particular profession or specific activity.

- Professional moral principles have led to ethical procedures specific to particular professions.
- An early source of ethics is the Hippocratic oath, a code of medical ethical behaviour that puts the patient's well-being first.
- Medical atrocities in the Nazi concentration camps of World War II led to the Nuremberg Code which governs the conduct of research on humans.
- Some researchers in the past did not follow normal ethical procedures, but justified their actions because of the understanding the research provided.

Ethics and research participants

Without a doubt, the ethical issues associated with participants in research take up the most time when you are planning and carrying out research. A number of points have already been mentioned earlier in this chapter but the following appear to be the most important ones that you should take into account during your research:

- informed consent
- right of refusal to take part, without penalty
- right to withdraw without penalty
- confidentiality and anonymity
- deception
- security and safety to prevent any emotional or physical harm.

Informed consent

Informed consent involves explaining the nature of the research to the participants so that they are in a position to make a decision about whether or not to take part. It is essential that you have some means to check that your potential participants do actually understand your explanations about what the research will entail. This of course raises a number of questions.

First, how much information should you provide to your participants? This raises the question: is it possible to provide *too much* information? You will also have to consider how much information is actually needed to enable the participants to feel comfortable about what they are letting themselves in for, to use a well-worn phrase.

There are a number of further questions to consider: how will you convey the information and explanation to the participants? Will you write to them? Will you provide them with an information sheet? Will you use telephone and/or email contact? The answers to these questions will, of course, depend on the kind of data collection you will use. A postal survey using a written questionnaire will necessarily need the inclusion of an explanatory letter and/ or information sheet that clearly and unambiguously explains the purposes and aims of the survey and the reasons for carrying it out.

A further issue concerns the covert collection of data. This is highly contentious. However, if this is a strategy that has been agreed for your research, then you will hardly want to ask for consent from your unknowing participants to collect the data.

Right of refusal to take part, without penalty

Participants should be given the opportunity to decline to take part in the research. In addition, it should be made clear that there is no penalty attached to not taking part. This should be explained to potential participants right at the very beginning, before the research gets underway. This becomes particularly important if the relationship between researcher and participants involves an asymmetry of power and/or authority. For example, if a student does not want to take part in research carried out by a teacher, they may feel that the teacher will think less of them or even discriminate against them in some way in the future.

Right to withdraw without penalty

Participants should also be given the right to withdraw at any time from the research once it is underway. Again, it should also be explicit in the information they receive that there is no penalty attached to withdrawing from the research.

Confidentiality and anonymity

Confidentiality and anonymity usually appear high on the list of ethical issues that researchers take into account in the way they manage their research participants. The main focus is on ensuring that neither participants nor their organisations are named at any stage in the research. In addition, the information you provide in your report should not enable participants to be identified.

Deception

Is it unethical to deceive your participants? This is a question that has exercised the minds of many researchers, especially since the publication of the Milgram experiments and other research that has included deception.

Homan (1991) discusses a number of examples from social science research that has involved deception, although he puts these under the heading of 'covert methods'. This, incidentally, indicates that at times it is difficult to separate out the different ethical categories. Among the examples he outlines from the published literature, include:

- 'Pseudo-patient studies' where, for example, a researcher posed as a psychiatric hospital patient;
- A white researcher who changed the colour of his skin to black to experience the prejudice and hostility that was rife in 1950s' America (this was mentioned earlier in Chapter 6);
- A doctoral student who became employed in a bakery in order to study work practices of the employees (and made the workers suspicious because of his 'ethnographer's bladder', since he secretly wrote up his field observations in the toilets);
- Observation of casual homosexual encounters where the researcher acted as a look out for strangers who might interrupt the activities taking place in the men's public toilets.

(Homan, 1991: see page 96 for more detail)

A dictionary definition of the term 'deceive' is: 'deliberately cause (someone) to believe something that is not true, especially for personal gain … give (someone) a mistaken impression' (Soanes and Stevenson, 2005: 449).

This definition implies there are two types of deception: intentional and unintentional. The above examples from Homan are illustrations of the former. As a researcher, you will know when you are using intentional deception: it will have been your decision to lie and be dishonest about what your research is about. These are strongly emotive words but they are an accurate description of the decisions you will have taken if you are tempted to use deception in your research.

It will be more difficult to know when unintentional deception is occurring. The risk of deceiving your participants in an unintentional manner raises questions about how much information you will need to give them and how much detail you will need to provide. It may not be feasible, or desirable, to spend a lot of time explaining exactly what your research is about. It may confuse and irritate the participants rather than reassure and enlighten them! At times it may be difficult to reach the right balance. But the golden rule should be: a little information is better than none and, at times, may be more preferable than too much.

Security and safety

Are you putting your participants in any danger or exposing them to any physical or emotional risk? The risk of emotional challenges during the data collection process will be present for research that covers sensitive or personal topics. Such research will no doubt require participants to engage emotionally, perhaps at a deep and significant level, with their experiences. If this is the case, then it is important for you to consider whether or not you are qualified and experienced enough to manage the feelings that may arise.

Depending on your approach to data collection, even the most unprovocative and uncontentious subjects for research may create emotional and personal difficulties for the participants. For example, imagine you are interviewing newly qualified social workers about the experience of starting work in their new profession. On the surface this is hardly an emotive topic. However, what if the informant is struggling with the pressures and demands of the work? What if they do not feel they can talk to their manager or any of their new colleagues? Further, what if there is no one outside of the workplace in whom they can confide? Your interview with them may be the first opportunity they have had to talk through their difficulties and it would be surprising if they did not unload their emotional issues on to you as you progress through the interview. It is not difficult to imagine that the interview situation in this instance could easily become a very challenging emotional experience for both of you.

The point of including this short scenario is to illustrate that an uncontentious subject for the researcher may turn out not to have the same emotional neutrality for the researched. In addition, you may also find it difficult to anticipate the participants' responses. For example, unbeknown to you, participants may derive some benefit from the experience of reflecting on and talking about their lives to a sympathetic listener (Elliott, 2005: 137).

It will be important, therefore, for participants to receive a clear explanation of what the research is about and the kinds of activities and/or questions that will form the basis of the data collection. In addition, participants should be provided with opportunities to ask for clarification or express any concerns or queries they may have about the research. This will not always result in the avoidance of the unpredictable arising, but it may help to reduce the possibility that you will be taken by surprise at the reactions of your participants.

Knowing what to do when difficulties do occur, however, demands being able to think on your feet and be responsive and sensitive to what is happening. For example, what should you do if 'information is disclosed during an interview which indicates that the participant is at risk of harm' (Ritchie and Lewis, 2003: 69)? In instances like this, it would be important for you to have a strategy for responding to the disclosure. For the vast majority of research, this will not arise. However, if your topic and focus of your research covers potentially personal and sensitive information, then you should be prepared, including having considered the following questions:

- Should you be concerned about the disclosure?
- Should you take responsibility for the disclosure since it occurred from one of the participants in *your* research?
- Will you inform someone outside of the research situation about the disclosure?
- Will you discuss it first with the participant before passing on any information?
- Will it be a betrayal of confidence – and therefore unethical – if you pass on the information without the permission of the participant?
- If you do not pass on the information and the participant harms him/herself, are you being unethical?
- Should you simply encourage the participants to seek help about whatever is concerning them?

At the very least, when such a disclosure occurs, you should take the opportunity of sharing your concerns with your supervisor or a senior member of the research team in your institution. What you should not do is take on the role of adviser or counsellor.

 Summary 12.2

- Among the most important ethical issues associated with participants in research are:

  – informed consent
  – right of refusal to take part, without penalty
  – right to withdraw without penalty

– confidentiality and anonymity
– deception
– security and safety to prevent any emotional or physical harm.

Conclusion

This chapter has focused on a number of important questions about the ethics of research and in particular those associated with how you should treat the participants in your research.

One very significant point that was mentioned is that sometimes there may be a conflict between different ethical principles. Sometimes a decision will lead to actions that are unethical in one respect but ethical in others. This is particularly the case when trying to balance the 'greater good' against individual need. If this occurs, then it will be important for you to be sensitive to the wider issues of the implications of your decisions. These wider issues can be seen against the different stages of the FraIM and the next chapter looks more closely at these.

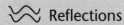 Reflections

1   What ethical issues will your research raise?
2   How will you address these particular issues?
3   What formal ethical procedures does your institution expect researchers to follow?
4   Can research that appears to be unethical ever be justified?

Associated reading

Associated reading about the ethics of social and educational research is included at the end of the next chapter.

Wider ethical issues and the FraIM

> **This chapter will:**
>
> - take a wider perspective of ethical issues that builds on the previous chapter
> - draw on ethical issues associated with other stages in the FraIM and not just the research participants
> - outline briefly the relationship between ethics, morals and values.

Introduction

The previous chapter explained the nature of ethics, why it is important and why you should take ethics into account in your research. In addition, it outlined the types of factors you will need to be aware of in relation to the participants in your research. This second chapter on ethics offers a wider perspective of ethical issues and highlights a number of factors associated with other stages in the FraIM and not just the research participants. It also discusses, briefly, the relationship between ethics, morals and values.

The research question

Developing an understanding of the ethical issues you may have to confront in your research starts, of course as you would expect, with the aims and focus of your research expressed through the research question. It may be apparent from the actual question itself that ethical problems may arise. Take the following example: *what are the effects of alcohol on the ability of 14–19-year-old students to navigate through information on selected web pages on the internet?*

This proposed research would raise obvious and serious implications not only for the conduct of the data collection but also the legality of supplying or condoning the consumption of alcohol by under-age drinkers. Ethically, it may be seen as indefensible to carry out such research. However, what if the question were: *what are the effects of alcohol on the ability of 14–19-year-old students to differentiate between acceptable and unacceptable social behaviour in mixed ethnic and mixed gender groupings?*

Would this proposed research be more ethically acceptable, since the outcomes may – at least at first sight – appear more commendable? Would the research be justifiable because potentially the outcomes could make a serious contribution to our understanding of the issues around social behaviour of young people under the influence of alcohol? You might want to argue that the findings could be used to influence policy decisions about alcohol availability and/or the education of young people, educationists, social services and law enforcement agencies. Is the research justifiable, therefore, despite the ethical challenges? The important point that is being made here is that your research question could very easily draw attention to many ethical problems that might arise during the research process.

Another dilemma that you may, at some point, have to deal with is if you make any changes to the original research question, the research aims and the focus of the research. If you *have* made any changes then ethically, when you write your research report, you should be honest about how these changed as the research developed.

Finally, you may want to consider whether or not there are any research questions or topics that, by implication, should not be pursued due to their inherently unethical nature?

Context

It is likely that your research will take place in a professional, organisational, policy and national context. Different contextual factors, therefore, will raise important ethical issues that you will need to be aware of and subsequently be able to address.

Professional context
The professional context will inevitably impose certain restrictions and make particular demands on your activities. Whether the context is, say, social work, education, health, nursing or the police, then how you manage your research will, in part, be determined by this context.

For example, within all professional contexts, the security and confidentiality of information will be paramount in your dealings with individuals and organisations. Specific codes of practice may be in place, too and you will be expected to adhere to these. The purpose of the codes will be to ensure that you follow the ethical principles and guidelines for undertaking research in that particular professional context. However, not all professional bodies have codes of practice that are specifically aimed at members undertaking research.

The GTCE (General Teaching Council for England) is the professional body for teaching in England. It has a Code of Conduct and Practice for Registered Teachers (General Teaching Council for England, 2009) but this does not include teachers undertaking their own research as part of their professional activities. The Code of Professional Standards for Police Officers, likewise, does not include guidance about research activities (Home Office, 2006).

On the other hand, the health services in the UK have sophisticated and relatively complex structures and procedures to deal with proposed research. Applications are made to local ethics committees which are part of the National Research Ethics Service (NRES). The NRES is part of the National Patient Safety Agency and its function is 'to protect the rights, safety, dignity and well-being of research participants and facilitate and promote ethical research that is of potential benefit to participants, science and society' (National Research Ethics Service, 2009).

The professional body for social workers, the BASW (British Association of Social Workers), has a code of ethics and this includes specific obligations on social workers who are engaged in research. One interesting clause in the code is the following, which states:

> Social work researchers will therefore ... Not use procedures involving concealment except where no alternative strategy is feasible, where no harm to the research subject can be foreseen and where the greater good is self-evidently served. (2002: 14)

This reflects Hammersley and Traianou's (2007) point mentioned earlier in Chapter 12 that, very often, ethical positions are in conflict with each other.

Professional associations

Professional associations that support specific subjects or disciplines also have their own code of ethics. Although these are not aimed at specific professional *vocations* or *locations*, nevertheless they can be considered to be associated with identified professional contexts and take place within a variety of particular professional locations. Examples of these are the British Psychological Association, the British Sociological Association, the British Educational Research Association, the American Psychological Association and the American Evaluation Association.

In addition, there are other bodies that are involved in research or provide funding for research that also expect codes of ethics to be followed. One example is the Economic and Social Research Council (ESRC) in the UK. The ESRC's research ethics framework points out that 'The ESRC does not seek to impose a detailed model for ethical evaluation and conduct on researchers or research organisations' (2005: 7) but it does expect minimum standards to be met.

Inter-professional working

One other important issue that you may have to consider is the demands of inter-professional research. If your research brings you into contact with a professional area with which you are unfamiliar or that you are not a member of, then you may find that the issues associated with 'insider' and 'outsider' research will work against you.

Gatekeepers may be suspicious of you as an outsider and may not feel it appropriate to allow you access to their professional context. This is not because they may question your methodological or intellectual competence, but because you do not have the professional socialisation experience which you can draw on in that particular context. Merton pointed out that in such a situation, the perception is that:

> the Outsider has a structurally imposed incapacity to comprehend alien groups, statuses, cultures and societies. Unlike the Insider, the Outsider has neither been socialized in the group nor has engaged in the run of experience that makes up its life, and therefore cannot have the direct, intuitive sensitivity that alone makes empathic understanding possible. (1972: 15)

Hellawell (2006) however, has pointed out that rather than there being two categories of researcher, there is in fact a continuum from insider to outsider researcher. When you undertake your research, you will be located somewhere on this continuum. You might also move backwards and forwards from one point to another on the continuum, depending on the nature of your research at any one particular time.

If you undertake research located in a profession with which you are unfamiliar, you will need to be sensitive to the ethical culture that pervades that profession. This observation also applies to carrying out research in an organisational context.

Organisational context

If your research is to take place in an organisation, then you will, of course, draw your participants from that organisation. You will need therefore to take into account a number of important issues. Consider your answers to the questions that follow in this section.

How will you gain access to the organisation, assuming you are not already a member? You will need to be honest about your research and why you are requesting access. Decision makers in the organisation who act as gatekeepers will expect you to explain your proposed research and will therefore no doubt assume that no deception is taking place.

If you are employing a sample of participants for your research, then how will you treat the remaining organisation members, assuming you come into contact with them?

How will you represent the organisation you are working with, outside of the organisation? Although you may not be a member of the organisation, you will be given a unique insight into the culture, activities and events taking place there. What will you say when you talk to others about the organisation? This, of course, is about trust. The organisation has allowed you access to its members. If you talk informally to others outside the organisation about what you witness, then is that an ethical position to take, especially if you are critical in what you say?

Another issue concerns research that draws on multiple locations. For example, if you intend to visit a number of schools in an area for your research, will you tell each school which other schools are involved in the research? If you do, then you will not be able to make any claims about anonymity, since people outside of one of your research locations will be aware of the identity of the other schools taking part. If you are asked by participants in one of the schools about which other schools are taking part in the research, then you will have to manage this request carefully and diplomatically.

How you behave therefore, before, during and after you visit an organisation will be important and will raise issues about confidentiality, trust and respecting the integrity of individuals in the organisation. There will also be the need to avoid any conflict of interest that may be potentially harmful to the research you are intending to carry out. Smythe and Murray explain that:

> Conflicts of interest generally arise from the potentially conflicting role that researchers can find themselves in when they also are involved with their participants in some capacity outside of the research, such as in therapy or in their personal lives. (2000: 315)

This involvement extends not just to the participants, but to those who are not participating in the research yet who are members of the organisation. For example, if the researcher knows a member of the senior leadership team in the organisation, say a school, where the research is being carried out, then should the sample of teachers being interviewed be made aware that the researcher is a friend of the senior member of the school? Would it be unethical *not* to tell the participants? This is not *quite* deception, but it *is* an example of the withholding of information.

Role of the researcher

In Chapter 6, it was suggested that there were ethical issues associated with the researcher's role. It was suggested that this role lay on a continuum, from full-observer (or researcher) through to observer/researcher-as-participant and participant-as-observer/researcher to full-participant. If you want to refresh your memory, the characteristics were outlined in Table 6.1.

Table 13.1 describes briefly the potential ethical pitfalls associated with each of the four main researcher roles.

Policy context

It was suggested in Chapter 2 that all research takes place in a policy context and is therefore inevitably political in nature (Clough and Nutbrown, 2002). This view has important implications for carrying out research. It suggests

Table 13.1   Examples of ethical issues and the researcher's role

Role	Brief description of example	Ethical issues
Full-observer	The researcher is sat at a desk in a university library noting the interactions between students using the computer terminals, without the students knowing they were being observed.	Should the researcher have been making notes about the students without their permission?
Observer-as-participant	The researcher visits a primary school and sits at the back of a classroom, noting down observations of teacher/pupil speech events.	Although the teacher and pupils were aware of being observed, did the observer explain fully what the research was about? Has permission been gained from the pupils' parents for the observations to be undertaken? Will the presence of the observer influence the lesson and will this be detrimental to the pupils' learning?
Participant-as-observer	A member of staff in a college of further education is collecting data by observing the senior leadership team, which has given permission for the observations.	Will issues of confidentiality arise if the focus of the discussion in the meetings concerns other staff members of the college?
Full-participant	A member of a senior leadership team is collecting data for a research project without the knowledge of the leadership team.	Should the researcher be carrying out observations without the knowledge of the team?

that you should be aware of any ethical or wider moral and political issues that might impinge on your research.

For example, your research might be about young people's attitudes to abortion. This can raise all sorts of sensitivities, prejudices and emotions that will need to be carefully managed. Many people will feel very strongly that abortion is immoral and any medical personnel involved are acting unethically. These views arise from the widely and firmly held values that underpin the cohesiveness of a society and its way of life.

Even a relatively uncontentious topic can reveal a wide range of associated ethical and political issues. For example, what about using mobile phones for text messaging? This is now a widespread phenomenon and many young (and older) people now use mobile phone technology to keep in touch with friends and family. Research has shown that 'Children who send or receive mobile messages (mobile e-mail or SMS) more frequently, tend to feel more strongly that their mobile phone is an essential tool in their life … Children think of mobile phones as "information gadgets" for communicating, particularly by mobile e-mail/SMS' (GSMA/NTT DOCOMO, 2009: 2). However, any research undertaken about the use of SMS (short message service) texts via mobile phones will inevitably raise questions about the use of technology in society, including its detrimental effects on the sociability of young people. Some New Zealand schools have banned the use of mobile phones because of fears of 'text bullying' and disruptions to school work (Thompson and Cupples, 2008: 95). This also used to be the case in the UK. However, in some areas, there is now a move to *encourage* students to use mobile phone technology to support their learning and to keep in touch with their families in case of emergencies (Hartnell-Young and Heym, 2008).

Research into the use of mobile technology by young people will therefore raise questions about a number of important and potentially contentious factors. These include policy decisions about the characteristics of schools in the future and the way the education system manages learning in schools, and provides support and security for young people.

These examples demonstrate that social and educational research does not take place in a social vacuum but draws, either explicitly or implicitly, on policy matters that have both moral and ethical implications.

National context

This also applies to the national context of research. All research is immersed in social and political cultures that will have an implicit and/or explicit impact on both researcher and participant. For example, imagine carrying out your research in a country that is challenging in terms of the standard of living of its people. That country may be, for example, Zimbabwe where, as you will know, there are serious social and economic problems due to the prevailing political situation. The situation in South Africa is very different from that in Zimbabwe, but carrying out research in South Africa can, nevertheless, be a challenging experience due to the tensions still prevalent post-apartheid.

A researcher working in these countries will always need to question whether or not it is morally acceptable to carry out the intended research. The question revolves around whether or not the research will be of benefit to anyone else apart from the researcher. This is obviously a question that is pertinent to all research, whatever the national context, but it is particularly acute when inter-cultural research is planned or the researcher is from a different country or culture.

For example, Plowright and Plowright (2008) carried out research in South Africa into community-based alternatives to formal education for orphaned and vulnerable children (OVCs) from a poor, rural black community. The authors argued that informal, community schooling programmes could be used to address poverty-based problems that are preventing South Africa's children becoming fully involved in education from an early age. They believed that this could be achieved through using a collaborative strategy to enable local government and NGOs (non-governmental organisations) to work closely with each other. However, the concluding remarks indicated that the authors were aware of the problems of using an ethno-centric perspective in the research:

[W]e need to be sensitive to our own position as concerned researchers, with a very different background to those we are researching. We are acutely aware of this and will need to continually ask ourselves if we are in danger of drawing on and imposing a western view of education policy on our research? (Plowright and Plowright, 2008: 9)

Another way of putting this is to state that research cannot be value-neutral. The national context within which any research takes place will draw on a range of social and cultural factors that will be associated with particular moral and ethical values. For example, in some countries gender segregation is a way of life that is underpinned by moral values that permeate those societies. In such a country, it would be unacceptable, for example, for a male researcher to propose research that involved interviewing female teachers or pupils in a girls' school. However, in the UK and the US, this would be normal practice. In other words, what is ethically acceptable in one country is not acceptable in another.

Theoretical context

The theoretical context or conceptual framework of your research will be based on the literature search and review that you will undertake for your research. It will provide the theories that will inform your research question, the interpretation of the findings and the overall conceptualisation and scholarly direction of your research. It will be drawn from the subject focus of your research.

Taking an ethical position will involve acknowledging 'any theoretical frameworks or value systems that may influence your interpretations and analysis' (Opie, 2004: 30). Taking an ethical position in relation to the conceptualisation of your research is also about honesty and avoiding deception, underpinned by your professional integrity as a researcher. This involves avoiding plagiarism and ensuring you acknowledge the sources of your information and ideas. There are a number of approaches you will need to bear in mind if you are to avoid plagiarism. Although these, strictly speaking, relate more directly to the writing and dissemination of your research report, it is appropriate to draw attention to them here. They include:

- only citing those publications that you have actually read
- acknowledging the source of your ideas and information, that means citing the publication from where you have taken the ideas and information, and then providing a reference for that source
- using quotation marks to indicate that the text is not your own, if you copy verbatim from a publication.

It is worth remembering that well-known saying that scholarly research is about standing on the shoulders of giants. This is very often attributed to the famous English physicist, mathematician and scientist, Sir Isaac Newton (1643–1727). The exact quotation, according to Maury was:

If I have seen further it is by standing on ye shoulders of Giants. (1992: 117)

All universities will have procedures that provide detailed information about avoiding plagiarism or 'unfair means' as it is often called. In the UK, these will be based on the Quality Assurance Agency for Higher Education's guidelines for enhancing the quality and standards of research programmes in universities (Quality Assurance Agency for Higher Education, 2004).

Summary 13.1

- A wider perspective of ethical issues draws on factors associated with each stage in the FraIM.
- The professional context will impose certain restrictions and make particular demands on your research activities.
- Visits to organisations require confidentiality and trust and respect for the integrity of individuals in the organisation.
- All social and educational research draws on policy matters that have moral and ethical implications.
- Acknowledge any theoretical frameworks or value systems that you have drawn on in your research.
- Avoid plagiarism by ensuring you acknowledge the sources of your information and ideas.

Methods of data collection

There will be a number of ethical issues associated with the data collection stage of your research. These are related partly to the way you treat the participants in your research and a number of examples of this have been discussed in the previous chapter.

In addition to the issues raised above, when you are asking questions of your participants, there is one further dilemma related to ensuring anonymity and confidentiality. What if, in the course of your research, an informant or participant gives you information that the law has been broken? What if that information concerns a child protection issue? Are you not morally, ethically and indeed legally bound to reveal that information to the proper authorities? This is where it is useful to plan ahead. You might need to ensure that the information you provide for the participants includes a 'disclaimer' about such situations. You could make it clear that if there is any disclosure of information that leads you to suspect that the law has been broken, then that information may be forwarded to the appropriate authorities.

When you carry out observations as part of your data collection, an important ethical issue concerns whether or not the observations are covert. Strictly speaking, informed consent should be gained before starting any observations, which of course rules out undertaking covert observation. However, what if your research involves observing, say, students' behaviour in the library as depicted in Table 13.1 or in your institution's coffee bars? Or in the examples discussed in Tables 6.3 and 6.4?

Your research may be about the use of non-verbal behaviour and in particular how people use personal space to negotiate relationships with those around them. If the participants knew you were observing their spatial behaviour, it is highly likely that it would change. As a full-observer does your role raise any ethical issues that need to be addressed?

If you are using artefact analysis to generate and collect the data for your research are there any ethical issues you may need to be aware of and take into account? Well, artefacts have been produced by other people and may, therefore, reflect their values and ideologies and maybe their prejudices and biases. The analysis of the MozVolunteers' web pages in Chapter 9 included a criticism of the organisation's approach to publicising its eco-friendly experience on the shores of the Indian Ocean. Although the authors agreed to the inclusion of the web pages in the book, the comments in Chapter 9 still challenge the perspective taken by those authors. The comments need to be sensitive to their efforts and their views. Both 'Alex' and 'Scott' are clearly committed to eco-friendly tourism and supporting the new clinic that provides a range of much-needed medical services for the local community.

Data and data analysis

There are issues linked with how you manage the data you have collected. Confidentiality and anonymity are important factors to take into account once the data have been collected, stored and are being analysed.

First of all, if you have recorded interviews as part of your research, you will need a strategy and procedure for ensuring that the recordings and the transcriptions are kept safe and secure and therefore confidential. The same applies to questionnaires and any other means you have used to record and store the data. There should be somewhere secure where you can keep discs, tapes, etc. At its simplest, this might be a lockable cupboard or draw where access is denied to anyone not involved in the research.

For electronic data, you will need to be confident that no one else has access to your computer and/or files. If you keep the data in your home, then what about the rest of your family or those you live with? You would be guilty of unethical practice if they can access any of the data that contains information that can identify the participants.

In addition to the above, the following should also be taken into account when planning your research:

- Where will you keep field notes, recordings, completed questionnaires and transcriptions?
- For how long will you keep field notes, recordings, completed questionnaires and transcriptions?

- Who else, apart from yourself, will have access to the information you have collected, including questionnaires with names and addresses?
- If you are not transcribing interviews yourself, what instructions will you give to the transcriber to ensure they do not share any of the information to which they have access?
- Who else will listen to the recordings?
- Who else will read the transcriptions?

Summary 13.2

- Decide what you will do if a participant indicates that the law has been broken.
- Informed consent should be gained before undertaking any data collection.
- Take into account that artefacts may reflect people's values and ideologies and maybe their prejudices and biases.
- Keep data safe and secure and therefore confidential.

Writing and disseminating the research report

One further point to make concerns the eventual writing and dissemination of your research report: it will be essential to write about the various ethical issues that you will have painstakingly paid attention to as you have planned and carried out your research. There will be an opportunity to include the documentation you have used, for example, about informed consent. This could also include the signed agreement forms from your participants.

In the way you write your research report, you will need to ensure that no individual or organisation can be identified. Bear in mind, too, that if you are required to place your final work in a university library then you will have the opportunity to request that an embargo is placed on it, if it contains sensitive information. This means that no one will be able to read it until after a specified period of time has passed, usually around three years.

You will also need to make it clear in your chapter or section on ethics that no deception has taken place and that the security and safety of your participants have been taken into account at all points in the research. Throughout the account, you will need to signal, through the choice of non-discriminatory language and style of writing, that you have afforded your participants a high level of respect.

If any of the above conditions have not been strictly adhered to, then you will have to demonstrate that there are very good reasons for not following expected ethical procedures. In addition, those reasons need to be explained carefully and in detail and include evidence of the authorisation from your organisation to undertake research that breaks normal ethical protocols.

> ### ☐ Summary 13.3
>
> - Include documentation in your report to support your claims that you have taken ethical issues into account in your research.
> - Ensure that no individual or organisation can be identified in your research report.
> - Signal, through non-discriminatory language and the style of writing, that you have afforded your participants a high level of respect.
> - Demonstrate that there are very good reasons if you have not followed ethical procedures, including evidence of the authorisation to undertake research that breaks normal ethical protocols.

A guiding framework

Finally, you will probably have realised by now that it is not always clear how to address some of the ethical dilemmas and situations you may confront in your research. As a guiding framework within the FraIM you may like to consider the following, although these suggestions, too, may have their difficulties.

- *Be available to explain the research to the participants before, during and after the data collection stages*: this will enable you to ensure that, as far as you are able, you can explain and clarify anything about the research that is causing or may cause concern, confusion or consternation to the participants at any time.
- *Put people first above all other considerations*: this will enable you to ensure that the participants are not exposed to any harm, embarrassment, harassment, humiliation, pain or deception as the research progresses.
- *Do unto others what you would like others to do unto you*: this may appear to be rather flippant, but it is a serious suggestion and is referred to as 'the golden rule'. It enables you to put yourself in the participants' position and gauge whether or not you would like to be exposed to those same conditions.
- *Participant-centred research*: at all times, the aim should be to carry out 'participant-centred research'. Using this particular ethic will entail the previous three factors and can be used as the overarching guiding principle on which your research should be based. The main principle is that of respect: respect for the people who are helping you by taking part in your research.

Summary of expected ethicality

Before your research is underway, you should undertake the following.

The research question

Provide a clear explanation of what the research will be about and the types of activities the participants will be asked to undertake and/or questions that the informants will be asked. Avoid using deception and provide honest, clear information.

Context

Ensure you are familiar with the codes of practice for your chosen professional context and for your university, college, etc. Complete any necessary ethical application before the data collection gets underway. Determine your role(s) as a researcher and consider the ethical implications of the chosen role(s).

Conceptualisation

Become familiar with your institution's requirements for citations and referencing, and ensure you read and understand your institution's plagiarism policy.

Participants

Provide an opportunity for the participants to ask for clarification or express any concerns or queries they may have before the data are collected. Provide opportunities for the participants to refuse to take part in the research, without penalty. Prepare informed consent forms for completion by the participants.

Methods of data collection

Plan and prepare for questions about the data collection procedures and consider including a disclaimer in the information for participants about breaking the law which would lead to information being passed on.

Data and data analysis

Plan and prepare for questions about the storage and use of data once collected.

Once your research is underway, you should follow the procedure below.

The research question

Be available to clarify the research to the participants during the data collection stages, especially if anything is causing confusion or consternation.

Context

Ensure you follow the particular codes of practice for your chosen professional context and for your organisation or institution. Ensure that organisational and individual confidentialities are maintained.

Conceptualisation

Be intellectually honest about the source of your ideas in any discussion or explanation about the research.

Participants

Provide ongoing opportunities for the participants to ask for clarification or express any concerns or queries they may have about the research. Ensure the participants can withdraw, without penalty, from the research without giving any reasons. Maintain confidentiality and anonymity for the participants, not only to those outside the organisation but, if necessary, to those within the organisation. Maintain conditions that provide security and safety for the participants to ensure they come to no physical or emotional harm. At all times, show respect, support and sensitivity to your participants in the way you talk *about* them and *to* them.

Methods of data collection

Do not discuss the research with anyone outside the organisation as the data collection gets under way to ensure that the organisation and/or individuals are not identified. Be sensitive to any discomfort or emotional difficulties the participants may be experiencing during the data collection stage.

Data and data analysis

Agree with the transcriber to sign a confidentiality agreement and keep the data secure once collected, including access by others, storage and length of time keeping data.

After your research has been completed, you should undertake the following.

The research question

Acknowledge and be honest about any changes you make to the original research question, research aims and focus of the research.

Context

Ensure that any actions that have been promised are carried out, for example, to send transcriptions or recordings. Ensure that nothing happens to alienate the research community or profession, that is, the profession should not be brought into disrepute (Homan, 1991: 172) by any unprofessional behaviour nor should it 'queer the pitch for other researchers' (Opie, 2004: 32).

Conceptualisation

Be intellectually honest about the source of your ideas after the research has been completed, especially when you write and produce your research report.

Participants

In any report, dissertation, thesis, journal or media article, web blog, etc., ensure that the organisation or individuals cannot be identified. Be responsive to any request for data to be withdrawn from inclusion in the research report. Follow up, however briefly, if a participant discloses that they are at risk of harm but do not take on the role of adviser or counsellor. Be prepared to refer participants to other support agencies if necessary. Continue maintaining respect and support for your participants if you have occasion to talk *about* them to colleagues and others outside the research.

Methods of data collection

Acknowledge, reflect on and learn from ethical mistakes that might have been made during the data collection stage of the research.

Data and data analysis

Keep all field notes, recordings, completed questionnaires and transcriptions secure for the stated length of time agreed and then destroy all materials after the agreed length of time has elapsed.

Writing and disseminating the research report

Ensure confidentiality and anonymity at all times. Use non-discriminatory language and images. Gain written permission from parents or guardians if using photographs of children in the report.

Conclusion

When you undertake research it is essential that you consider, in some detail, the ethical issues you will confront. This applies to all research. Whatever the research question, the context, the data source management, methods or type of data, you will be expected to be aware of and act on the ethical demands of your research. Undertaking research using the FraIM demonstrates that such demands are not restricted to the research participants: they permeate all stages of the research process, including the presentation of the final report.

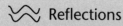

Reflections

1 What ethical problems might you encounter as a result of the role you will take during your research?

2 Draw up an action plan to show how you will manage the ethical issues associated with your methods of data collection and analysis. Use something similar to the table below:

Research activity	Issue	Why it's an issue	Action to be taken to ensure ethicality

3 Are there any ethical considerations that might prevent you from undertaking your research?

Associated reading 📖

- Alderson, P. and Morrow, V. (2004) *Ethics, Social Research and Consulting with Children and Young People.* Ilford: Barnardo's.
- Buchanan, E.A. (ed.) (2004) *Readings in Virtual Research Ethics: Issues and Controversies.* London: Information Science Publishing.
- Campbell, A., Charlesworth, M., Gillett, G. and Jones, G. (1997) *Medical Ethics.* Oxford: Oxford University Press.
- Farrell, A. (2005) *Ethical Research with Children.* Buckingham: Open University Press.
- Homan, R. (1991) *The Ethics of Social Research.* London: Longman.
- Jacob, J.M. (1988) *Doctors and Rules.* London: Routledge.
- Johns, M.D., Chen, S.S. and Hall, G.J. (2004) *Online Social Research: Methods, Issues and Ethics.* Oxford: Peter Lang.
- Milgram, S. (1974) *Obedience to Authority: An Experimental View.* London: Tavistock.
- Zimbardo, P. (2007) *The Lucifer Effect: How Good People Turn Evil.* London: Rider.

Holistic integrationism: philosophising research

> **This chapter will:**
> - discuss the role of philosophy in research methodologies
> - enable you to consider whether or not you need to use a philosophical framework in your own research
> - present an integrated paradigmatic framework associated with the FraIM.

Introduction

There is an ongoing debate about the underlying philosophical issues that, many argue, should give direction to educational and social research. You may have already encountered these arguments. You may also have been intrigued by the level and intensity of disagreement about some of the ideas you will have come across. There is not the space in this book to go into these debates in any great depth, perhaps unfortunately, since the arguments are really quite fascinating. However, at the end of this chapter you will find a number of suggestions for further reading if you become seriously interested in these issues. Beware though – they can become rather addictive!

The arguments are based on two important philosophical subjects: ontology and epistemology.

Ontology is 'the philosophical investigation of the nature, constitution and structure of reality' (Audi, 1999: 563). It can also be described as the theory of being or of what exists (Cardinal, Hayward and Jones, 2004). It asks the question: 'what is the world really made of?' (Moses and Knutsen, 2007: 5). In other words, ontology is about the inescapable and ultimate reality that we are all part of.

Epistemology, on the other hand, is concerned with knowledge and belief about reality (Dancy, 1985). This is echoed in Cardinal, Hayward and Jones's explanation that epistemology is the theory of knowledge and it attempts 'to provide humans with beliefs about the true nature of reality' (2004: 1). Epistemology is also about how we arrive at our knowledge, about how our knowledge *originates*. More importantly for research, it is about how we can *justify* the truth of the beliefs that we hold. In terms of the FraIM, epistemology is concerned with the justification for the claim that your knowledge or belief is warrantable. This was covered in Chapter 11.

Paradigms

A basic, underlying argument about the link between philosophy and research tends to be polarised between what are referred to as 'paradigms' (Kuhn, 1996). A paradigm is a system of ideas or theoretical principles that determine, maintain and reinforce our way of thinking about an issue or a topic. It is a set of basic beliefs that are accepted on faith with no way of establishing their ultimate truthfulness (Guba and Lincoln, 1998: 200).

Traditionally, the paradigms that underpin research are seen as being bipolar opposites. These are, on the one hand, the so-called scientific, naturalist tradition, and on the other, a constructivist paradigm. The former is also referred to as positivism although strictly speaking we are currently in a post-positivist period.

Put briefly, a scientific, naturalistic paradigm argues that the world we inhabit has an ontological reality, an existence that is not dependent on our perception, understanding or descriptions of that reality or world. It is referred to as being mind-independent. Reality is 'out there', that is, outside of us and exists even when there are no humans to perceive and experience that reality. It is an objective reality in which facts about the world are 'universal': that is, there are facts that are true for me and those same facts are also true for you. Boghossian gives the example of Jupiter's moons:

> [T]he fact that Jupiter has over thirty moons is a universal fact – it does not vary from person to person or community to community. (2007: 13)

The scientific paradigm is often referred to as having an ontologically realist perspective of the world. A constructivist paradigm, in contrast, claims that reality is mind-dependent and is socially constructed through the relationships, psychological activities and shared understandings that we all take part in. But in contrast with the first paradigm, a constructivist paradigm tends to be interested in *social* reality, which is:

> somehow generated by the way we think or talk about it, by our consensus about its nature, by the way we explain it to each other and by the concepts we use to grasp it. (Collin, 1997: 2–3)

Boghossian points out that 'the fact that there is money in the world is not a mind-independent fact – money could not have existed without persons and their intentions to exchange goods with one another' (2007: 13). The money has been given meaning and exchange value because people have built such a system into their lives. Unlike the moons of Jupiter, money did not exist before people came on the scene. However, the facts of money are not necessarily true for you and true in the same way for me. Therefore, working within a constructivist paradigm means that the characteristics of this social world are determined by people's subjectivities. It is not an objective world that is mind-independent; it is a world that would not exist without people. In epistemological terms, our knowledge of this world, inevitably, is also socially constructed.

Two realities?

This raises an important question. Should we, in fact, talk of there being *two* realities? On the one hand there is the spatio-temporal, natural world of objects – for example, the moons of Jupiter. On the other hand, there is the social world of ideas, relationships and institutions that are the products of human social and psychological experiences – for example, money?

Bhaskar explains that the natural world is an *intransitive* reality that is not dependent on the ability of human beings to mentally or socially construct that world (Sayer, 2000). It is *a priori* – it is an ontologically prior intransitive reality, which means that the world had a prior existence before people came along and experienced that world and conceptualised its characteristics. The world was there to be discovered and understood.

By contrast, the social world is a *transitive* reality. It is not a permanent world that endures over time and space with the same unchanging characteristics, since it is a product of human agency. It is *a posteriori* – it is an ontologically posteriori transitive reality. The social world is constructed through experience and thus has an existence only after people conceptualise its characteristics. However, the social world is contained within and constrained by the natural world. By this is meant that the social world depends on and draws from the natural world for its existence and its many characteristics. People are part of both worlds. The social world cannot exist without the natural world. (At this point you may want to consider whether or not the natural world can exist without the human or social world?)

In your research, however, you will be interested in developing an understanding of the social and educational issues important to the focus of your investigation. Therefore, your interests will be firmly located within the field of *social* epistemology (Fuller, 2002) rather than on the more general questions that philosophers might want to raise about knowledge.

Polarised paradigms

Even though your particular interest is in social epistemological issues, you will still need to consider whether or not we can study the social world in the same way that we study the spatio-temporal world of objects. There is still a raging debate about whether or not we can research this social world using a scientific methodology. Such methodology is, of course, appropriate for studying chemicals and biological and physical phenomena. But is it appropriate for investigating the structures and process that form the transitive *social* world?

This debate however is not just about methodology. It has its source in the different traditionally polarised ontologies that view reality as either mind-independent or mind-dependent. Many argue this has led to the opposing paradigms within which research is carried out. These traditional paradigms are seen as incompatible. This is because ontological reality cannot be both mind-dependent *and* mind-independent. Logically, it has to be either one or the other. Therefore, your ontological assumptions and beliefs will, it is argued, constrain the epistemology you subscribe to, which in turn will determine the research methodology you employ (Guba and Lincoln, 1998). Furthermore, Grix argues that:

> we need to realise that we can't chop and change between ontologies and epistemologies as we see fit, because (a) many combinations are not logical and (b) … your research foundations are a skin, not a sweater to be changed every day. (2004: 57)

This logically leads to the decision that you will not be able to integrate different approaches in your research. But in practical terms, this is exactly what happens on a regular basis. Indeed, chapters in this book have shown you *how* to do this. So, whatever the theory or philosophy appears to say, integration of different approaches *does* occur and occurs very successfully. This could mean, for example, that either the underpinning philosophical arguments *can* be reconciled and used together or they are not relevant to undertaking research. The former view can be supported by referring to research that relies on a paradigmatic pluralism, where different methodologies are successfully deployed. The alternative view, that philosophical arguments are not relevant to determining methodological strategies, can be supported by referring to research whose methodology does not appear to be driven by either of the traditional philosophical perspectives.

Philosophy is not relevant?

There is a further argument for the view that philosophy is not relevant to methodology. In fact, it is not so much the lack of relevance, but the *inappropriateness* of philosophical theory to decisions about practical research methodology. This is related to the view, explained above, that the study of the social sciences should be based on the scientific model of research. Here, theory plays an important role. Indeed, scientific and technological advances are almost synonymous with the development of scientific *theory*. Such theoretical developments are then applied to various contexts, including different technologies.

As an example, take a very simple theory applied to the study and use of electricity, that of Ohm's law. This states that the voltage of an electric circuit is equal to the current divided by the resistance in a circuit. It is represented by the following formula:

$$V = \frac{I}{R}$$

V = voltage; I = current; R = resistance

The application of electrical theory to many areas of technology is based on this simple formula. For example, when you turn on a dimmer switch for a light in a room, the brightness of the bulb will increase as you turn the dial. This is because the switch mechanism is constructed so that as you turn the dial, the resistance of the circuit in the switch decreases. Equations should always balance, so since V=I/R and the voltage remains the same, the values of I will increase. More current will flow through the circuit, including the light bulb. More current will result in increased brightness. The theory predicts the outcome. Constructing a dimmer switch in a particular way must therefore be determined, as well as explained, by the theory, by Ohm's law. If the theory is ignored when the dimmer switch is made, either it will not work or if it does, then it will work by chance because you will have correctly wired it up by chance.

But can you apply this approach to the *philosophical* theories that are supposed to determine the practicalities of your research? If you work within a scientific, naturalist paradigm, then according to a traditional view, your research approach will be predetermined. So, if your approach does not fit, if you do not adhere to the dictates of the theory, then your research will not work. But what does that mean? That you will not be able to contact your respondents? Collect and analyse the data? It does not actually make much sense to treat philosophical theorising in the same way that such theorisation is employed in the natural sciences. But this is what a traditional approach to research demands and this is what some writers expect you to do.

Paradigmatic reconciliation?

What about the other alternative, that the paradigms *can*, in philosophical terms, be reconciled and used together? Logically, different ontological assumptions *are* incompatible. However, this assumes that the reality being referred to in each case is the same reality. It was mentioned above that there are two types of reality: the transitive and the intransitive. The world of intransitive objects is a realist world that is mind-independent while the transitive, social world is mind-dependent. The transitive is contained in and constrained by the intransitive. Is this a sensible and intelligent way of looking at this issue? Does this, in fact, resolve the problem about lack of compatibility? At this point you may want to reflect on this and in addition apply these ideas to your own research.

☐ Summary 14.1

- According to a traditional view, research methodology is determined by philosophical perspectives.
- Traditional bipolar paradigms are referred to as naturalism and constructivism.
- These paradigms are usually seen as being incompatible with each other.
- Alternative views claim that the paradigms:

  – are actually compatible, as different methodologies are successfully used in research
  – are not relevant to making decisions about methodology, since not all research is driven by philosophical theories and the use of theory in research is based on a scientific model that is not appropriate for social science research.

A more radical possibility

There is however another, more radical, possibility that you might want to consider. This can be expressed in the following way:

> Philosophy does not determine the research methodology employed. It's the other way round: methodology determines the philosophy you might employ to explain your approach to undertaking research.

This fourth perspective may appear rather unusual and is not one that you would necessarily have come across previously. It is the view that you are invited to apply when you use the FraIM as the basis of your research. This view argues that philosophies are theories about the world and theories enable us to understand better our decisions, perspectives and activities when we deal with the world. They provide a framework for understanding our current perspective in relation to issues with which we are currently engaged.

Theories are constructed after an event and are developed through the process of induction. Observations take place, then theorisation attempts to make sense of the observations. Subsequent observations are then explained by reference to the theory. In turn, observations are used to test or check the accuracy of the theory through a process of deduction.

The problem here is that often more than one theory or explanation can be used to explain the evidence. For our purposes, this means that a philosophical theory is in competition with other philosophical theories, or paradigms, to provide an explanation for the methodology used in research. Yet no one perspective or paradigm is the correct one. As Guba and Lincoln (1998) point out: the philosophical debates would have been resolved a long time ago if we could unequivocally say that one and only one philosophical explanation is able to provide us with the ultimate truth.

We choose between paradigms to explain and justify our choice of research methodology. The methodology comes first, determined by the research question. Then, the chosen paradigm provides a theoretical structure or framework that enables us to offer a coherent and cohesive explanation for the decisions we have made. But the paradigm does not *determine* the approach we take since, as Williams and May point out, 'Philosophy might have the capacity to illuminate, but it hardly dictates' (1996: 135). Another way of putting this is to argue that it does not prescribe, nor legislate for, the methodology used in research (Delanty and Strydom, 2003).

So, what paradigmatic characteristics, therefore, are associated with the FraIM?

An alternative paradigm

Not surprisingly, the paradigm employed by the FraIM is based on an integrated perspective underpinning the research process. It relies heavily on an alternative and more recently developed philosophy that appears to be highly appropriate to explaining the underpinning principles and processes of the FraIM: pragmatism.

Pragmatism was a reaction against a traditional perspective of what was seen as misleading and unhelpful explanations of knowledge. This traditional approach argued that there is a difference between *knowing* something and *believing* something about the world in which we live.

There is a wealth of argument, example and (inevitably) contention about how we can justify claiming that our beliefs are true. The arguments that knowledge is *justified true belief* demonstrate that philosophers are interested in knowledge which gives us a certainty about the world. They are also interested in the *source* of this certain knowledge. Historically and traditionally answers to this question are based on two main perspectives: rationalism and empiricism. Rationalism argues that our knowledge comes from logic, mathematics, intuition and reasoning. Baggini points out that 'Such reasoning does not depend upon the data of experience, but proceeds from basic truths which do not require to be and are not grounded in experience' (2002: 11). In contrast, empiricism argues that our knowledge of the world is derived from sense data, that is, the information we acquire from our senses as we see, hear, taste, smell and touch the world around us, as was pointed out in Chapter 6.

Both empiricism and rationalism attempt to provide a reliable foundation of knowledge on which all other knowledge is based. This is why they are often referred to as *foundationalist* perspectives. Foundationalism involves a search for beliefs that need no further justification by referring to other beliefs. Rationalists use reason and logic as the foundation of true beliefs whereas empiricists argue that the foundation of all true beliefs is sense data.

Foundationalism relies on the process of regression to identify the chain of beliefs that is the justification for other beliefs. For example, if I am stranded in the desert without water, then I believe I may die of dehydration. My belief is based on other beliefs which have led me to my rather disturbing and worrying conclusion. One belief justifies another belief, as in the following:

I believe I may not survive because I am at risk of dehydration.
I believe I am at risk of dehydration because I do not have any water.
I believe I do not have any water because I have drunk all my water.
I believe I have drunk all my water because I am very thirsty.
I believe I am very thirsty because I am perspiring profusely.
I believe I am perspiring profusely because the temperature is 45 degrees Celsius.
And so on.

The statements are of course answers to continually asking the question: 'why?' The underlying purpose is to develop knowledge that gives us a true and accurate understanding of the reality we are studying. It aims to produce a full knowledge of the world that corresponds to and is identical with that world. In order words, it is a correspondence theory of truth which you came across in Chapter 11. A statement is true if it accurately and truthfully describes or corresponds to the world we are studying.

Both rationalism and empiricism aim to identify our most fundamental beliefs that require no justification, no further beliefs. These beliefs will form the foundations on which all other beliefs will rest and on which all other beliefs depend. Once we know what the fundamental beliefs are, then we have certain knowledge about the world. Another way of putting this is to say that these fundamental or foundational beliefs are *self-justifying*.

For the traditional empiricist, the foundations of knowledge rest on the aspiration to give an accurate account of how things appear to be. As far as the rationalists are concerned, Descartes' famous saying 'I think therefore I am' provides a foundational belief that needs no further justification, cannot be doubted, is certain and can be described as being self-evident. Foundational beliefs can therefore be described as being *infallible*.

It is questionable, however, whether or not we can *ever* arrive at an infallible or certain knowledge of reality, whatever perspective we take or whatever we believe our understanding to be. Which is where the pragmatists enter the picture. Pragmatism argues that the truth is 'what works'. This is perhaps a rather clumsy phrase but it encapsulates the main idea of this alternative – and more useful – paradigm.

Pragmatism is usually associated with three American philosophers: Charles Peirce (1839–1914), William James (1842–1910) and John Dewey (1859–1952). (You have already come across C.S. Peirce in Chapter 8). Inevitably, these three do not necessarily agree on all aspects of this particular philosophy but the main focus of a pragmatist view is that justification of a belief is dependent on how successful its practical consequences are. Another way of putting this is to say that pragmatism relies on the *consequences* of our beliefs. This is in contrast to foundationalism which relies on the *antecedents* of our beliefs. Antecedents are beliefs that precede our current beliefs and enable us to arrive at justified true beliefs or certain knowledge.

Pragmatism argues that if statements about the world do not lead to consequences or actions that are instrumental in enabling us to make appropriate decisions, take effective action and successfully get things done, then those statements or beliefs will not count as knowledge. To describe this state of affairs, Dewey (1941) referred to the *warranted assertability* of our claims to knowledge. This is a way of arriving at true statements about the world which result from successful inquiry. You read about this in Chapter 11, which looked at Toulmin's (1958) *The Uses of Argument* as the basis of undertaking valid research.

In addition, pragmatism takes both a relativist and a fallibilist view of what knowledge is. In other words, it rejects the idea that we can ever arrive at a final and unequivocal understanding of the world and its characteristics. This means that beliefs are 'work in progress' and therefore are subject to change, amendment and revision. Knowledge and understanding, therefore, are neither static nor certain.

A summary of the above points is shown in Figure 14.1.

An integrated framework for research

These ideas are acknowledged in the alternative paradigm on which the FraIM draws and within which you might comfortably locate your research. This alternative paradigm consists of:

- a pragmatic integrated methodology
- a relativist social epistemology
- a realist social ontology
- a realist object ontology.

This approach is referred to as holistic integrationism. It employs a pragmatic, integrated methodology to undertake investigations using empirical (or sense) data from observation, asking questions and artefact analysis. The process begins with the research question. The intended outcome will be to arrive at the warranted assertability of your research conclusions, thus enabling you to engage successfully with the social and educational issues that are the focus of your research.

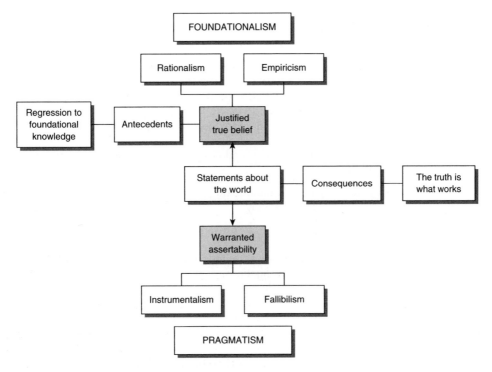

Figure 14.1   Contrasting foundationalism with pragmatism

Working within the FraIM, a pragmatic methodology invites you to carry out research that has a purpose, that is aimed at informing decisions and activities that impact on the world or that solve problems. It is highly appropriate for carrying out social and educational research that is useful and enables you to 'get things done'. So it follows that you will not be expected to start your research with a discussion of the underpinning theories that characterise your own philosophical position. These do not drive the research: it is the research question that will determine the approach you take.

Your aim will be to arrive at the warranted assertability of your knowledge claims. This will be achieved by drawing on a relativist social epistemology which accepts that as our knowledge and understanding of the world develop and change, then what works will, over time, also change. The world we are trying to understand is characterised by an ontologically posteriori transitive reality that consists of the selected social structures and processes you are interested in for your research.

Ontologically, the nature and characteristics of this world are restrained and constrained by the spatio-temporal world of objects and processes that characterise an ontologically prior intransitive reality. To put this more simply, an object ontology puts boundaries around what is possible in a social ontology. It restricts what we are able to do and the way we are able to live and experience the social and material world of which we are all a part.

Summary 14.2

- Paradigms provide a theoretical structure or framework that enables us to offer a coherent and cohesive explanation for the decisions we have made.
- The FraIM argues that methodology determines the philosophy used to understand approaches to undertaking research.
- Philosophy, therefore, does not prescribe, or legislate for, the methodology used in research.
- The FraIM is based on an integrated paradigmatic framework for research, consisting of:

  – a pragmatic integrated methodology
  – a relativist social epistemology
  – a realist social ontology
  – a realist object ontology.

- This approach is referred to as holistic integrationism and is based on undertaking empirical investigations.

Conclusion

In this chapter you have been introduced to an important debate in the use of research methodologies. Unfortunately, there is only the space to touch on this debate in a very brief and almost cursory fashion. The important point to take away from this chapter, however, is that when you use the FraIM in your research you should bear in mind that philosophy does not determine the methodology you employ. As you have seen, it is the other way round: the methodology leads to the selection of a philosophical perspective that enables you to explain and therefore understand better the methodology you have used. On this occasion, you are encouraged to draw on a pragmatic methodology, a relativist social epistemology that is fallibilist and instrumentalist, and realist ontologies to explain your approach.

Reflections

1 Consider whether or not social science can use the same methodologies that are used in the natural sciences.
2 What are your views about a paradigmatic perspective on research? Are the traditional paradigms:

- incompatible
- reconcilable
- not relevant to research?

> 3 What are your views about an integrated paradigm, where the methodology leads to the philosophical perspective, rather than the converse?
>
> 4 Use an integrated paradigm to describe and explain your own research.

Associated reading

- Baggott, J. (2005) *A Beginner's Guide to Reality*. London: Penguin.
- Boghossian, P. (2007) *Fear of Knowledge: Against Relativism and Constructivism.* Oxford: Clarendon Press.
- Bryman, A. (1988) *Quantity and Quality in Social Research*. London: Routledge.
- Dewey, J. (1941) 'Propositions, warranted assertibility, and truth', L.A. Hickman and T.M. Alexander (eds) (1998), in *The Essential Dewey, Volume 2: Ethics, Logic, Psychology*. Bloomington: Indiana University Press.
- Gage, N.L. (1989) 'The paradigm wars and their aftermath: a "historical" sketch of research on teaching since 1989', *Educational Researcher*, 18 (7): 4–10.
- Greene, J.C. and Caracelli, V.J. (2003) 'Making paradigmatic sense of mixed methods practice', Chapter 3 in A. Tashakkori and C. Teddlie (eds), *Handbook of Mixed Methods in Social and Behavioral Research*. London: SAGE.
- James, W. (1907) *Pragmatism: A New Name for Some Old Ways of Thinking: Popular Lectures on Philosophy*. London: Longmans, Green.
- O'Brien, D. (2006) *An Introduction to the Theory of Knowledge*. Cambridge: Polity.
- Peirce, C.S. (1934) *Collected Papers of Charles Sanders Peirce: Volume 5: Pragmatism and Pragmaticism*. Edited by C. Hartshorne and P. Weiss. Cambridge, MA: Harvard University Press.
- Phillips, D.C. and Burbules, N.C. (2000) *Postpositivism and Educational Research*. Oxford: Rowan & Littlefield.
- Pring, R. (2000) *Philosophy of Educational Research* (2nd edn). London: Continuum.
- Rosenberg, A. (2005) *Philosophy of Science: A Contemporary Introduction* (2nd edn). London: Routledge.
- Teddlie, C. and Tashakkori, A. (2009) *Foundations of Mixed Methods Research: Integrating Quantitative and Qualitative Approaches in the Social and Behavioral Sciences*. London: SAGE. See Chapter 5, 'Paradigm issues in mixed methods research'.
- Williams, M. and May, T. (1996) *Introduction to the Philosophy of Social Research*. London: Routledge.

15

A few final words

This chapter will:

- provide a brief summary of the main characteristics of the FraIM
- identify two important concepts on which the FraIM is based
- point out that the FraIM can be used for any type of social and educational research, and not just a mixed methods approach
- encourage you to use an integrated methodology as the basis for carrying out your own research.

An integrated methodology

This book has introduced a new way of thinking about social and educational research using an integrated methodology. It has provided a structure that is referred to as the FraIM: frameworks for an integrated methodology. It is a development of the mixed methods approach to undertaking research and as such, builds on many ideas already available in the published literature. However, what is different about the FraIM is the bringing together of these different ideas to provide a main framework within which rest a number of sub-frameworks. These frameworks create a supporting structure for thinking anew about how we conceptualise and carry out social and educational research. To begin with, research starts with a research question which subsequently determines the strategies, approaches and activities that are used to successfully complete a research project.

All research takes place in a number of different contexts. These are the professional, organisational, policy, national and theoretical contexts. You may feel that there is room for a further contextualisation of your research and this is the international or global context in which your research will be undertaken. Globalisation issues are having an increasing impact on the way we think and behave, and in your research there may be the opportunity to draw on your understanding of these issues.

Whatever your research, you will need to decide on what your cases, or sources of data, will be. The FraIM has a two-stage process that enables you to think through first, the data source management, and, second, the case sampling strategy you will use. The aim is to make an appropriate selection of cases that will provide you with the empirical data for your research. Such data will be collected using one or more methods of data collection: observation, asking questions and artefact analysis. Working within the FraIM enables you to draw on two important characteristics of these methods: level of mediation, a 'between-methods' characteristic, and degree of structure, a 'within-methods' characteristic. Degree of structure is a commonly used criterion to distinguish different approaches from each other. However, you may not have come across the idea of level of mediation before reading this book. It is an under-developed idea that should reward further work into developing a more sophisticated concept that can be applied to collecting data.

The FraIM refers to narrative and numerical data. Again, both these terms are in common usage but not perhaps in relation to describing the basic distinction between the types of data collected during research. That is, of course, if there is a distinction to be made. The process of data transformation suggests the differences are not so clear-cut. That also applies to the analysis of data you will undertake in your research. You may be tempted to analyse numerical data mathematically and produce a more discursive response to analysing narrative data. Depending on your research question and what you hope to discover, you may decide to analyse numerical data in a discursive manner and subject the narrative data to a mathematical analysis.

However you approach the data collection and analysis, your aim will be to produce the evidence on which the claims about your cases will be made. This will enable you to make warrantable inferences that will lead to a valid conclusion to your research and will allow you to answer your research question.

Conceptual considerations

The above has summarised, very briefly, the FraIM. Conceptually it is associated with two strands. The first is the increasing amount of material and discussion around the use of mixed methods in social and educational research. The second is the philosophical debate about the use of a paradigmatic approach to undertaking research.

In relation to the first, Tashakkori and Creswell, in the very first edition of the *Journal of Mixed Methods Research*, defined the area as 'research in which the investigator collects and analyzes data, integrates the findings, and draws inferences using both qualitative and quantitative approaches or methods in a single study or a program of enquiry' (2007: 3).

In this book, you have seen that the FraIM takes a comprehensive position on mixed methods, or more accurately, an integrated methodology. It provides a framework that can be used to structure thinking and activities to achieve warrantable research that holistically integrates all stages of the research process.

It firmly rejects a commonly used and traditional nomenclature to describe research. It argues that such terms, the 'Q' words, are obstacles to developing the practice of using an integrated methodology. As a doctoral student said in one of my recent classes, such an approach is 'liberating'. It frees the mind from the constraints of the past and points the way to the future.

The second strand that the FraIM draws on is that of the debate over the links between philosophy and methodology. This was discussed, all too briefly, in Chapter 14. Very often, such a discussion appears early in a book about research methods. In this book, it appears towards the end. This was a deliberate decision, to reflect the argument that philosophy does not determine methodology: methodology determines the philosophy you might employ to explain (or maybe even rationalise?) your approach to undertaking research.

Working within the FraIM encourages a more integrated way of thinking about the links between philosophy and methodology. This still assumes, of course, that these links exist and are important for the decision-making process when carrying out research. The FraIM draws on a pragmatic, integrated methodology; a relativist social epistemology and realist social and object ontologies. You may have found that the argument here was under-developed. If you did, then I suspect your observations are justified since there is more work to be done about this aspect of the FraIM. Despite this, it may not be too premature to use the term 'holistic integrationism' to describe such an approach. It may not be an ideal label, but it is a start at trying to make sense of the kaleidoscope of ideas that are used in this particular field of study.

So, finally ...

You are now familiar with the main framework and the sub-frameworks that make up the FraIM. I hope you have found a lot that you like and that you can use in your own research.

The title of the book is *Using Mixed Methods: Frameworks for an Integrated Methodology*. Ironically, but not surprisingly, the FraIM can be used for any type of social and educational research. It doesn't necessarily have to be about 'mixing' methodologies. Perhaps that suggests that all research has a common link, a common basis, whatever the tradition or history it draws on. That link is about undertaking systematically planned research that has a socially useful purpose and is based on an holistic integrationist strategy to achieve warrantable outcomes.

The FraIM aims to make a small contribution to that endeavour.

References

Alderson, P. and Morrow, V. (2004) *Ethics, Social Research and Consulting with Children and Young People*. Ilford: Barnardo's.

Audi, R. (ed.) (1999) *The Cambridge Dictionary of Philosophy* (2nd edn). Cambridge University Press: Cambridge.

Baggini, J. (2002) *Philosophy Key Themes*. Basingstoke: Palgrave Macmillan.

Baggott, J. (2005) *A Beginner's Guide to Reality*. London: Penguin.

Barthes, R. (1993) *Image, Music, Text: Essays Selected and Translated by Stephen Heath*. London: Fontana.

Bassey, M. (1999) *Case Study Research in Educational Settings*. Buckingham: Open University Press.

Bell, J. (2002) 'Questionnaires', in M. Coleman and A.R.J. Briggs (eds), *Research Methods in Educational Leadership*. London: SAGE.

Belsey, C. (2005) 'Textual analysis as a research method', in G. Griffin (ed.), *Research Methods for English Studies*. Edinburgh: Edinburgh University Press.

Bentham, J. (1843) *The Works of Jeremy Bentham, Published under the Superintendence of His Executor, John Bowring Volume IV*. Edinburgh: William Tait.

Berelson, B. (1952) *Content Analysis in Communication Research*. Hafner: New York.

Bergman, M.M. (ed.) (2008) *Advances in Mixed Methods Research*. London: SAGE.

Blaikie, N. (2000) *Designing Social Research*. Cambridge: Polity.

Blaxter, L., Hughes, C. and Tight, M. (2006) *How to Research* (3rd edn). Maidenhead: Open University Press.

Boghossian, P. (2007) *Fear of Knowledge: Against Relativism and Constructivism*. Oxford: Clarendon Press.

Bourner, T. (1996) 'The research process: four steps to success', in T. Greenfield (ed.), *Research Methods: Guidance for Postgraduates*. London: Arnold.

Boyle, D. (2000) *The Tyranny of Numbers*. London: HarperCollins.

Brimblecombe, N. and Ormston, M. (1995) 'Teachers' perceptions of school inspection: a stressful experience', *Cambridge Journal of Education*, 25 (1): 53–61.

British Association of Social Workers (2002) *The Code of Ethics for Social Work*. Birmingham: the British Association of Social Workers. Available at: www.basw.co.uk/Portals/0/CODE%20 OF%20ETHICS.pdf

British Medical Journal (1996) 'Nuremberg doctors' trial: the Nuremberg Code (1947)', *British Medical Journal*, 313 (7070), 7 December: 1448. Available at: www.bmj.com/cgi/content/ full/313/7070/1448

Bryman, A. (1988) *Quantity and Quality in Social Research*. London: Routledge.

Bryman, A. (2008) *Social Research Methods* (3rd edn). Oxford: Oxford University Press.

Bryman, A. and Cramer, D. (2009) *Quantitative Data Analysis with SPSS 14, 15 and 16: A Guide for Social Scientists*. London: Routledge.

Buchanan, E.A. (ed.) (2004) *Readings in Virtual Research Ethics: Issues and Controversies*. London: Information Science Publishing.

Burgess, H., Sieminski, S. and Arthur, L. (2006) *Achieving Your Doctorate in Education*. London: SAGE.

Burton, N., Brundrett, M. and Jones, M. (2008) *Doing Your Research Project*. London: SAGE.

Bush, T. (2002) 'Authenticity – reliability, validity and triangulation', in M. Coleman, and A.R.J. Briggs (eds), *Research Methods in Educational Research*. London: SAGE.

Cameron, D. (2001) *Working with Spoken Discourse*. London: SAGE.

Campbell, A., Charlesworth, M., Gillett, G. and Jones, G. (1997) *Medical Ethics*. Oxford: Oxford University Press.

Cardinal, D., Hayward, J. and Jones, G. (2004) *Epistemology: the Theory of Knowledge*. London: Hodder Murray.

Chandler, D. (2002) *Semiotics: The Basics*. Routledge: London.

Charmaz, K. (2006) *Constructing Grounded Theory: A Practical Guide through Qualitative Analysis*. London: SAGE.

Clough, P. and Nutbrown, C. (2002) *A Student's Guide to Methodology*. London: SAGE.

Cobley, P. and Jansz, L. (2004) *Introducing Semiotics*. Royston: Icon Books.

Cohen, L., Manion, L. and Morrison, K. (2007) *Research Methods in Education* (6th edn). London: Routledge.

Collin, F. (1997) *Social Reality*. London: Routledge.

Coolican, H. (2004) *Research Methods and Statistics in Psychology* (4th edn). London: Hodder Arnold.

Coyle, A. (2007) 'Discourse analysis', in E. Lyons and A. Coyle (eds) *Analysing Qualitative Data in Psychology*. London: SAGE.

Creswell, J. (2003) *Research Design: Qualitative, Quantitative and Mixed Methods Approaches* (2nd edn). London: SAGE.

Creswell, J.W. (2007) *Qualitative Enquiry and Research Design: Choosing Among Five Approaches* (2nd edn). London: SAGE.

Creswell, J.W. and Plano Clark, V.L. (2007) *Designing and Conducting Mixed Methods Research*. London: SAGE.

Culler, J. (1988) *Saussure*. Hassocks: Harvester Press.

Dancy, J. (1985) *Introduction to Contemporary Epistemology*. Oxford: Blackwell.

Deacon, D., Pickering, M., Golding, P. and Murdock, G. (2007) *Researching Communications* (2nd edn). London: Hodder Arnold.

Dean, J. (1995) 'What teachers and headteachers think about inspection', *Cambridge Journal of Education*, 25 (1): 45–52.

Delanty, G. and Strydom, P. (eds) (2003) 'Introduction: what is the philosophy of science?', in *Philosophies of Social Science: the Classic and Contemporary Readings*. Maidenhead: Open University Press.

Dewey, J. (1941) 'Propositions, warranted assertibility, and truth', in L.A. Hickman and T.M. Alexander (eds) (1998), *The Essential Dewey, Volume 2: Ethics, Logic, Psychology*. Bloomington: Indiana University Press.

DfES (2003) *Every Child Matters*. Norwich: Stationery Office.

Dickens, C. (2003) *Hard Times*. Harmondsworth: Penguin.

Economic and Social Research Council (2005) *Research Ethics Framework*. Swindon: ESRC. Available at: www.esrcsocietytoday.ac.uk/ESRCInfoCentre/Images/ESRC_Re_Ethics_Frame_tcm6-11291.pdf

Eisner, E. (1993) 'Objectivity in educational research', in M. Hammersley (ed.) *Educational Research: Current Issues*. London: Paul Chapman.

Elliott, J. (2005) *Using Narrative in Social Research: Qualitative and Quantitative Approaches*. London: SAGE.

Fairclough, N. (1995) *Critical Discourse Analysis: The Critical Study of Language*. London: Longman.

Fann, K.T. (1970) *Peirce's Theory of Abduction*. Martinus Nijhoff: The Hague.

Farrell, A. (2005) *Ethical Research with Children*. Buckingham: Open University Press.

Field, A. (2005) *Discovering Statistics Using SPSS* (2nd edn). London: SAGE.

Finch, H. and Lewis, J. (2003) 'Focus groups', in J. Ritchie and J. Lewis (eds), *Qualitative Research Practice: A Guide for Social Science Students and Researchers*. London: SAGE.

Fink, A. and Kosecoff, K. (1998) *How to Conduct Surveys: A Step-by-Step Guide*. London: SAGE.

Fogelman, K. (2002) 'Surveys and sampling', in M. Coleman and A.R.J. Briggs (eds), *Research Methods in Educational Leadership*. London: SAGE.

Fuller, S. (2002) *Social Epistemology* (2nd edn). Bloomington: Indiana University Press.

Gage, N.L. (1989) 'The paradigm wars and their aftermath: a "historical" sketch of research on teaching since 1989', *Educational Researcher*, 18 (7): 4–10.

Gibson, James J. (1986) *The Ecological Approach To Visual Perception*. London: Lawrence Erlbaum.

Gilbert, N. (2001) *Researching Social Life* (2nd edn). London: SAGE.

Gillham, B. (2005) *Research Interviewing: The Range of Techniques*. Maidenhead: Open University Press.

Gomm, R., Hammersley, M. and Foster, P. (2000) *Case Study Method*. London: SAGE.

Gorard, S. (2002) 'Fostering scepticism: the importance of warranting claims', *Evaluation and Research in Education*, 16 (3): 136–49.

Gorard, S. and Taylor, C. (2004) *Combining Methods in Educational and Social Research*. Maidenhead: Open University Press.

Gottdiener, M. (1995) *Postmodern Semiotics: Material Culture and the Forms of Postmodern Life*. Oxford: Blackwell.

Greene, J.C. and Caracelli, V.J. (2003) 'Making paradigmatic sense of mixed methods practice', in A. Tashakkori and C. Teddlie (eds), *Handbook of Mixed Methods in Social and Behavioral Research*. London: SAGE.

Griffin, J.H. (1977) *Black Like Me* (2nd edn). Boston: Houghton Mifflin.

Grix, J. (2004) *The Foundations of Research*. Basingstoke: Palgrave MacMillan.

General Teaching Council for England (2009) *Code of Conduct and Practice for Registered Teachers*. London: General Teaching Council for England. Available at: www.gtce.org.uk/133031/133036/139476/139482/code_of_conduct_1009.pdf

GSMA/NTT DOCOMO (2009) *Children's Use of Mobile Phones: An International Comparison*. GSM Association/NTT DOCOMO. Available at: http://emergingtechnologies.becta.org.uk/index.php?section=etr&catcode=ETRE_0001&rid=14390

Guba, E.G. and Lincoln, Y.S. (1998) 'Competing paradigms in qualitative research', in N.K. Denzin and Y.S. Lincoln (eds), *The Landscape of Qualitative Research*. London: SAGE.

Guiraud, P. (1975) *Semiology*. London: Routledge.

Halfpenny, P. (1997) 'The relation between quantitative and qualitative social research', *Bulletin de Methodologie Sociologique*, 57: 49–64. Available at http://bms.sagepub.com/cgi/reprint/57/1/49

Hall, S. (2001) 'Foucault: power, knowledge and discourse', in M. Wetherell, S. Taylor and S.J. Yates (eds) *Discourse Theory and Practice: A Reader*. London: SAGE.

Hammersley, M. (1992) *What's Wrong with Ethnography?* London: Routledge.

Hammersley, M. and Atkinson, P. (1995) *Ethnography: Principles in Practice*. London: Routledge.

Hammersley, M. and Traianou, A. (2007) *Ethics and Educational Research*. London: TLRP. Available at: www.tlrp.org/capacity/rm/wt/traianou

Haney, C., Banks, W.C. and Zimbardo, P.G. (1973a) 'A study of prisoners and guards in a simulated prison', *Naval Research Reviews*, 9: 1–17. Available at: www.zimbardo.com/downloads/1973%20A%20Study%20of%20Prisoners%20and%20Guards,%20Naval%20Research%20Reviews.pdf

Haney, C., Banks, W.C. and Zimbardo, P.G. (1973b) 'Interpersonal dynamics in a simulated prison', *International Journal of Criminology and Penology*, 1: 69–97.

Hartnell-Young, E. and Heym, N. (2008) *How Mobile Phones Help Learning in Secondary Schools: A Report to Becta*. Nottingham: University of Nottingham. Available at: http://emergingtechnologies.becta.org.uk/index.php?section=etr&catcode=ETRE_0001&rid=14128

Hellawell, D. (2006) 'Inside-out: analysis of the insider-outsider concept as a heuristic device to develop reflexivity in students doing qualitative research', *Teaching in Higher Education*, 11 (4): 483–94.

Henle, M. and Hubbell, M. (1938) 'Egocentricity in adult conversation', *The Journal of Social Psychology*, 9 (2): 227–34.

Hodson, R. (1999) *Analyzing Documentary Accounts*. London: SAGE.

Holsti, O.R. (1969) *Content Analysis in the Social Sciences*. Reading, MA: Addison-Wesley.

Holloway, I. and Freshwater, D. (2007) *Narrative Research in Nursing*. Chichester: Blackwell.

Homan, R. (1991) *The Ethics of Social Research*. London: Longman.

Home Office (2006) *New Code of Professional Standards for Police Officers*. London: Home Office. Available at: www.homeoffice.gov.uk/documents/police-code-consultation

Hopkins, D. (2002) *A Teacher's Guide to Classroom Research* (3rd edn). Buckingham: Open University Press.

Hudson, P. (2005) 'Numbers and words: quantitative methods for scholars of texts', in G. Griffin (ed.), *Research Methods for English Studies*. Edinburgh: Edinburgh University Press.

Hume, L. and Mulcock, J. (2004) *Anthropologists in the Field: Cases in Participant Observation.* New York: Columbia University Press.

Huysman, M. (1999) 'Balancing biases: a critical review of the literature on organizational learning', in M. Easterby-Smith, J. Burgoyne and L. Araujo (eds), *Organizational Learning and the Learning Organization.* London: SAGE.

Jacob, J.M. (1988) *Doctors and Rules.* London: Routledge.

James, W. (1907) *Pragmatism: A New Name for Some Old Ways of Thinking: Popular Lectures on Philosophy.* London: Longmans, Green.

Johns, M.D., Chen, S.S. and Hall, G.J. (2004) *Online Social Research: Methods, Issues and Ethics.* Oxford: Peter Lang.

Johnstone, B. (2002) *Discourse Analysis.* Blackwell: Oxford.

Junker, B.H. (1960) *Field Work: An Introduction to the Social Sciences.* London: University of Chicago Press.

Knight, P. (2002) *Small-Scale Research.* London: SAGE.

Krippendorff, K. (2004) *Content Analysis: An Introduction to its Methodology* (2nd edn). London: SAGE.

Kuhn, T.S. (1996) *The Structure of Scientific Revolutions* (3rd edn). Chicago: University of Chicago Press.

Legard, R., Keegan, J. and Ward, K. (2003) 'In-depth interviews', in J. Ritchie and J. Lewis (eds), *Qualitative Research Practice: A guide for Social Science Students and Researchers.* London: SAGE.

Likert, R. (1932) 'A technique for the measurement of attitudes', *Archives of Psychology*, 22 (140): 5–55.

Lonsdale, P. and Parsons, C. (1998) 'Inspection and the school improvement hoax', in P. Earley (ed.), *School Improvement after Inspection? School and LEA Responses.* London: Paul Chapman.

Lyons, E. and Coyle, A. (eds) (2007) *Analysing Qualitative Data in Psychology.* London: SAGE.

MacLure, M. (2003) *Discourse in Educational and Social Research.* Maidenhead: Open University Press.

Mann, C. and Stewart, F. (2003) 'Internet interviewing', in J.F. Gubrium and J.A. Holstein (eds), *Postmodern Interviewing.* London: SAGE.

Maury, J. (1992) *Newton: Understanding the Cosmos.* London: Thames & Hudson.

Merton, R.K. (1972) 'Insiders and outsiders: a chapter in the sociology of knowledge', *The American Journal of Sociology*, 78 (1): 9–47.

Milgram, S. (1963) 'Behavioral study of obedience', *Journal of Abnormal and Social Psychology*, 67 (4): 371–8.

Milgram, S. (1974) *Obedience to Authority: An Experimental View.* London: Tavistock.

Moses, J.W. and Knutsen, T.L. (2007) *Ways of Knowing: Competing Methodologies in Social and Political Research.* London: Palgrave McMillan.

Moyles, J. (2002) 'Observation as a research tool', in M. Coleman and A.R.J. Briggs (eds), *Research Methods in Educational Leadership.* London: SAGE.

Muijs, D. (2004) *Doing Quantitative Research in Education with SPSS.* London: SAGE.

National Research Ethics Service (2009) www.nres.npsa.nhs.uk/aboutus/about-nres/how-we-work/

Neuendorf, K.A. (2002) *The Content Analysis Guidebook.* SAGE: London.

Nöth, W. (1995) *Handbook of Semiotics.* Indiana University Press: Bloomington & Indianapolis.

O'Brien, D. (2006) *An Introduction to the Theory of Knowledge.* Cambridge: Polity.

Ofsted (2004) *Standards and Quality 2002/03: The Annual Report of her Majesty's Chief Inspector of Schools.* London: Ofsted.

Onwuegbuzie, A.J. and Johnson, R.B (2006) 'The validity issue in mixed research', *Research in the Schools*, 13 (1): 48–63. Reproduced in V.L. Plano Clark and J.W. Creswell (eds) (2008), *The Mixed Methods Reader.* London: SAGE.

Opie, C. (ed.) (2004) *Doing Educational Research: A Guide to First Time Researchers.* London: SAGE.

Oppenheim, A.N. (2000) *Questionnaire Design, Interviewing and Attitude Measurement.* London: Continuum.

Palaiologu, I. (2008) *Childhood Observation.* Exeter: Learning Matters.

Parker, I. (1999) *Critical Textwork: An Introduction to Varieties of Discourse and Analysis.* Buckingham: Open University Press.

Pedler, M., Burgoyne, J. and Boydell, T. (1991) *The Learning Company: A Strategy for Sustainable Development.* London: McGraw-Hill.

Peirce, C.S. (1932) *Collected Papers of Charles Sanders Peirce, Volume 2: Elements of Logic.* Edited by C. Hartshorne and P. Weiss. Cambridge, MA: Harvard University Press.

Peirce, C.S. (1934) *Collected Papers of Charles Sanders Peirce, Volume 5: Pragmatism and Pragmaticism.* Edited by C. Hartshorne and P. Weiss Cambridge, MA: Harvard University Press.

Pell, A. and Fogelman, K. (2002) 'Analysing quantitative data', in M. Coleman and A.R.J. Briggs (eds), *Research Methods in Educational Leadership.* London: SAGE.

Pellegrini, A.D. (2004) *Observing Children in their Natural Worlds: A Methodological Primer* (2nd edn). Mahwah, NJ: Lawrence Erlbaum.

Phillips, D.C. and Burbules, N.C. (2000) *Postpositivism and Educational Research.* Oxford: Rowan & Littlefield.

Pink, S. (2007) *Doing Visual Ethnography: Images, Media and Representation in Research* (2nd edn). London: SAGE.

Plano Clark, V.L. and Creswell, J.W. (2008) *The Mixed Methods Reader.* London: SAGE.

Plantinga, A. (2008) 'Warrant: a first approximation', in E. Sosa, J. Kim, J. Fantl, and M. McGrath (eds), *Epistemology: An Anthology* (2nd edn). London: Blackwell.

Plowright, D. (1991) 'Context, text and reader: understanding communications technology through television advertisements'. Unpublished PhD thesis.

Plowright, D. (2007) 'Self-evaluation and Ofsted inspection: developing an integrative model of school improvement', *Educational Management, Administration and Leadership*, 35 (3): 373–93.

Plowright, A. and Plowright, D. (2008) 'Developing identities in South Africa: alternatives to formal schooling for disadvantaged black children'. Paper presented at the CCEAM Conference, Think Globally Act Locally: A Challenge to Education Leaders held in Durban, South Africa. Available at: www.emasa.co.za/files/full/A%20Plowright%20&%20D%20Plowright.pdf

Potter, J. (2004) 'Discourse analysis as a way of analysing naturally occurring talk', in D. Silverman (ed.), *Qualitative Research: Theory, Method and Practice.* London: SAGE.

Pring, R. (2000) *Philosophy of Educational Research* (2nd edn). London: Continuum.

Punch, K.F. (2006) *Developing Effective Research Proposals.* London: SAGE.

Punch, K.F. (2009) *Introduction to Research Methods in Education.* London: SAGE.

Quality Assurance Agency for Higher Education (2004) *Code of Practice for the Assurance of Academic Quality and Standards in Higher Education. Section 1: Postgraduate Research Programmes* (2nd edn). Gloucester: QAA.

Rhodes, S.D. (2004) 'Hookups or health promotion? An exploratory study of a chatroom-based HIV prevention intervention for men who have sex with men', *AIDS Education and Prevention*, 16 (4): 315–27.

Ritchie, J. and Lewis, J. (2003) *Qualitative Research Practice: A guide for Social Science Students and Researchers.* London: SAGE.

Robson, C. (2002) *Real World Research* (2nd edn). Oxford: Blackwell.

Rorty, M.V., Mills, A.E. and Werhane, P.H. (2007) 'Institutional practices, ethics and the physician', in R. Rhodes, L.P. Francis and A. Sivers (eds), *The Blackwell Guide to Medical Ethics.* Oxford: Blackwell.

Rosenberg, A. (2005) *Philosophy of Science: A Contemporary Introduction* (2nd edn). London: Routledge.

Rose, G. (2007) *Visual Methodologies: An Introduction to the Interpretation of Visual Materials* (2nd edn). London: SAGE.

Salkind, N.J. (2008) *Statistics for People Who (Think They) Hate Statistics* (3rd edn). London: SAGE.

Sanger, J. (1996) *The Compleat Observer? A Field Research Guide to Observation.* London: Falmer Press.

Saunders, L. (1999) 'Who or What is School "Self"-Evaluation for?', *School Effectiveness and School Improvement*, 10 (4): 414–29.

Saussure, F. de (1972) *Course in General Linguistics*. Edited by Bally, C. and Sechehaye with the Collaboration of Riedlinger, A., Translated by Harris, R. London: Duckworth.

Sayer, A. (2000) *Realism and Social Science*. London: SAGE.

Senge, P.M. (1990) *The Fifth Discipline: the Art & Practice of The Learning Organization*. London: Random House Business Books.

Shannon, D.M., Johnson, T.E., Searcy, S. and Auburn, A.L. (2002) 'Using Electronic Surveys: Advice from Survey Professionals', *Practical Assessment, Research and Evaluation*, 8 (1). Available at http://PAREonline.net/getvn.asp?v=8&n=1

Silverman, D. (2006) *Interpreting Qualitative Data* (3rd edition). London: SAGE.

Simmons, R. (2001) 'Questionnaires', in N. Gilbert (ed) *Researching Social Life* (2nd edn). London: SAGE.

Smythe, W.E. and Murray, M.J. (2000) 'Owning the story: ethical considerations in narrative research', *Ethics and Behaviour*, 10 (4): 311–336.

Soanes, C. and Stevenson, A. (eds) (2005) *Oxford Dictionary of English* (2nd edn, revised). Oxford: Oxford University Press.

Stevens, S.S. (1946) 'On the theory of scales of measurement', *Science*, 103 (June): 677–680.

Tashakkori, A. and Creswell, J.W. (2007) 'Editorial: The New Era of Mixed Methods', *Journal of Mixed Methods Research*, 1 (1): 3–7.

Tashakkori, A. and Teddlie, C. (eds) (2003) *Handbook of Mixed Methods in Social and Behavioral Research*. London: SAGE.

Tashakkori, A and Teddlie, C. (2008) 'Quality of inferences in mixed methods research: calling for an integrative framework', in M.M. Bergman (ed) *Advances in Mixed Methods Research*. London: SAGE.

Teddlie, C. and Tashakkori, A. (2009) *Foundations of Mixed Methods Research: Integrating Quantitative and Qualitative Approaches in the Social and Behavioral Sciences*. London: SAGE.

Thompson, L. and Cupples, J. (2008) 'Seen and not heard? Text messaging and digital sociality', *Social and Cultural Geography*, 9 (1): 95–108.

Toulmin, S.E. (1958) *The Uses of Argument*. Cambridge: Cambridge University Press.

Trafford, V. and Leshem, S. (2008) *Stepping Stones to Achieving Your Doctorate*. Maidenhead: OU Press.

Velleman, P.F. and Wilkinson, L. (1993) 'Nominal, ordinal, interval and ratio typologies are misleading', *The American Statistician*, 47 (1): 65–72.

Wetherell, M. (2001) 'Themes in discourse research: the case of Diana', in M. Wetherell, S. Taylor and S.J. Yates (eds) *Discourse Theory and Practice: A Reader*. London: SAGE.

Wetherell, M., Taylor, S. and Yates, S.J. (eds) (2001) *Discourse Theory and Practice: A Reader*. London: SAGE.

Whyte, W.F. (1993) *Street Corner Society: The Social Structure of an Italian Slum* (4th edn). Chicago: University of Chicago Press.

Williams, M. and May, T. (1996) *Introduction to the Philosophy of Social Research*. London: Routledge.

Wodak, R. and Meyer, M. (2001) *Methods of Critical Discourse Analysis*. SAGE: London.

Woodruff, S.I., Conway, T.L., Edwards, C.C., Elliott, S.P. and Crittenden, J. (2007) 'Evaluation of an Internet virtual world chat room for adolescent smoking cessation', *Addictive Behaviors*, 32: 1769–86.

Wragg, E.C. (1999) *An Introduction to Classroom Observation* (2nd edn). London: Routledge.

Wragg, T. (2002) 'Interviewing', in M. Coleman and A.R.J. Briggs (eds), *Research Methods in Educational Leadership*. London: SAGE.

Yin, R.K. (2003a) *Applications of Case Study Research*. London: SAGE.

Yin, R.K. (2003b) *Case Study Research: Design and Methods* (3rd edn). London: SAGE.

Zimbardo, P.G. (1973) 'On the ethics of intervention in human psychological research: with special reference to the Stanford Prison Experiment', *Cognition*, 2 (2): 243–56.

Zimbardo, P. (2007) *The Lucifer Effect: How Good People Turn Evil*. London: Rider.

Name Index

Subject Index